HIGH PERFORMANCE HIRING

Robert W. Wendover

A FIFTY-MINUTE™ SERIES BOOK

CRISP PUBLICATIONS, INC.
Menlo Park, California

HIGH PERFORMANCE HIRING

Robert W. Wendover

CREDITS
Editor: **Nancy Shotwell**
Typesetting: **Interface Studio**
Cover Design: **Carol Harris**
Artwork: **Scott Sewell**

Distribution to the U.S. Trade:

National Book Network, Inc.
4720 Boston Way
Lanham, MD 20706
1-800-462-6420

Library of Congress Catalog Card Number 90-84078
Wendover, Robert W.
High Performance Hiring
ISBN 1-56052-088-4

CONTENTS

INTRODUCTION

THE COMPLEXION OF HIRING IS CHANGING

The character of hiring has changed! Employers used to place an ad in the paper or a sign in the window and receive a stack of applications the next day. This no longer happens.

With the changes in applicants' attitudes and experience, businesses cannot count on traditional sources of labor. For instance, women will represent almost half of those entering the work force, and Hispanics another 35 percent.

These changes have brought a host of considerations the employer must make before filling an opening. Successful businesses are finding that day-care options, flextime and maternity leave are benefits that must be provided to keep the best performers. Bi-lingual and basic skills training must be provided to maintain a productive work force.

Many individuals entering the work force today lack the basic skills and work ethic so prevalent in earlier generations. Employers can no longer assume that applicants possess even the most basic competencies required for business. If American companies are to thrive in the years ahead, they will need to begin training at a significantly lower level. While some firms are taking this initiative, most are still searching for workers who possess the needed skills. Organizations must cultivate new sources of labor and commit to a program of training that will satisfy their future needs. This practice, coupled with skilled leadership and motivation, will result in a productive and loyal work force.

Not only must you find people with skills, you must find people who have the desire to work. Today, the average worker's attention is drawn in many directions. Getting individuals to produce the level of work needed to keep your company competitive is one of the crucial challenges of the next decade.

To begin this process, you must first examine your present hiring procedures and philosophy. As a good recruiter evaluates more than what an applicant says, applicants need to examine how the hiring process is conducted. Employee selection cannot be a one-sided event.

THE HIRING SKILLS INVENTORY

To examine the procedure in your organization, consider the following hiring skills inventory. These questions address the major considerations of a successful hiring effort.

1. *Have you defined the type of person who excels in your organization?*

Examine the culture: What motivates your top performers? How well do people get along? Is this a serious atmosphere or perhaps a more fun-loving? How important are people skills in your business?

Make a list of the characteristics you think are needed to be successful in your organization. Pass it around to others and ask them to add their thoughts. The resulting factors can comprise a checklist for what to look for in your new hires.

2. *Are your hiring procedures consistent and well-defined?*

Employee selection that is conducted without clear procedures or performed in a haphazard way can result in high turnover, discrimination, or loss of your best applicants. Hiring need not be a complicated process, but it must have direction. Hiring must also be conducted with consistency. If candidates are treated in a variety of ways, they will be confused and frustrated. A clearly defined and timely succession of steps results in a positive impression among your top candidates.

3. *Is everyone involved well-informed?*

Often, too many people are involved in the hiring process. It does not take six people to hire a receptionist. A few key people should be responsible for screening applicants and making timely decisions.

Those screening individuals should know job description, selection procedures, time table and regulations regarding the selection process. Do not assume that even high-level managers are adept at hiring. Take the time to make sure this important process is explained to everyone.

4. *Are you tracking recruiting costs?*

How much did it cost to replace the last receptionist who left the organization? With employee turnover running into thousands of dollars, no organization can afford to be sloppy with its hiring. Calculating turnover and recruiting costs will bring home the seriousness of conducting employee selection with care.

Figure 1—Sample memo on turnover

MEMORANDUM

TO: Anne Clark, General Manager
FROM: Steve Elliott, Human Resources

I broke down our expenses for replacing the hourly workers we keep turning on the 320 line. The figures even surprised me. We need to do something about this!

Last shift (exit interview, cleaning out locker, etc.) 4 hours @ $10 (including benefits)	$40.00
Termination paperwork 1 hour @ $12	12.00
Recruiting new hire (including advertising, interviews, orientation, etc.) 6 hours @ $12	72.00
Training New hire's unproductive time 8 hours @ $10 (w/benefits) Trainer's time 15 hours @ $13 (over one week)	80.00 195.00
	$399.00

We went thru this 17 times last quarter to the tune of $6,783 or $27,132 per year!

---

5. *Are you continually cultivating new sources of applicants?*

A number of companies have watched the bottom fall out of their applicant pools because of the diminishing numbers of high-school-age workers. Technical managers are also scrambling because of the lack of skilled craftsmen.

The development of new and consistent sources of labor requires going outside traditional resources. You cannot wait for one source to dry up before pursuing another. The public relations and marketing you do in your community should include recruiting. Applications should be tracked and candidates should be queried about how they learned of positions.

THE HIRING SKILLS INVENTORY
(Continued)

Figure 2—Sample recruiting report

RECRUITING REPORT			
Position title _____		Number of openings _____	
Sources			
Type	**Cost of using source**	**Yield**	**Comments**
In-house posting			
Classified ads			
Employee referrals			
Agency (private)			
Agency (public)			
Other			
General recommendations: _____			

6. *Are you considering the versatility of candidates?*

While most people are hired to perform one role, many end up doing a variety of tasks. Are you looking for individuals who readily adapt to new responsibilities and challenges?

7. *Are you studying your competitors' recruiting techniques?*

Do you know what those organizations are doing to locate applicants? How are they retaining the best performers? Look for their advertisements. Talk to your own employees who have worked for them. Listen closely at professional and industry meetings. Try to figure which of their ideas would work for you.

8. *Are you "the employer" to work for?*

Have you developed a reputation in town as an organization that treats its employees well? Is the word on the street that people working for you succeed? This type of public relations goes a long way toward both attracting applicants and retaining employees. You want your employees to be proud of where they work. Learn to sell your best candidates on how working for you can be a good move for them.

9. *Are you hiring "10's"?*

Are you and your managers stretching yourselves by hiring the best people available? Too many times managers tend to hire good followers as opposed to good potential leaders. While this strategy will make their lives easier in the short run, it also can hinder the growth of the organization. Impress upon managers that hiring those with the drive to succeed will not only improve the company, it will make them look good.

10. *Are you properly orienting new employees?*

Think back to when you entered this organization: How were you welcomed? Was someone there to assist you with the intricacies of completing forms and learning the ropes?

What do you do for new hires to insure that they receive a good first impression? A little investment in helping them adapt will lead to loyalty and a desire to work hard.

While this checklist is not all inclusive, it should give you a working knowledge of the key components in hiring. Notice that they are not all mechanical. They involve focus, philosophy and a general understanding of human nature. Selection processes that are too mechanical neglect the understanding needed to select not only the qualified person, but the right person for the job.

HOW TO USE THIS BOOK

The average person receives little or no training on how to select employees. While there are a number of books available on the secrets of interviewing, this is only one part of the process. *High Performance Hiring* is designed to equip you with the tools necessary to select the best candidates available.

Acquiring the skills to become a competent recruiter involves more than just reading this book. Take the time to develop hiring procedures that work for you. There are no rules to follow other than having a focus on what you're looking for and concentrating on selecting the best applicants.

To best use *High Performance Hiring*, read it through and make note of those areas where you need the most assistance. Then go back and concentrate on the highlighted sections to get to know them better. There are plenty of examples and forms. Adapt these to your needs. The more you feel comfortable with the process, the more effective you will be in hiring.

WHAT ARE YOU LOOKING FOR?

ROLE OF JOB AUDITS AND DESCRIPTIONS

We often view the writing of job descriptions as a boring task, but these documents form the backbone of an organization's structure.

Job descriptions serve two vital purposes. First, they provide definition, parameters, and a feel for the role positions play within the greater organization. Second, they serve as bench marks for measuring performance.

It is not uncommon for an agency investigating a labor claim to ask for a job description as part of its investigation. Written job descriptions are not required by law, but organizations that do not have up-to-date descriptions may seem unmindful of their employees' rights and responsibilities.

The traditional job description includes needed skills and qualifications along with tasks and duties. The new, cutting-edge job description takes more personal factors into consideration.

Factors such as the pace of the job and ability to deal with people have as much of an influence on job success as technical skills. While you cannot specify discriminatory requirements such as ''attractive woman'' in a description for restaurant host, you can explain that the position requires an enthusiastic personality and someone who is able to deal with a wide variety of customers. In another case, such as service representative, you can specify that applicants must be perseverant, since they will have to track down complicated problems.

There is no more uncomfortable feeling than not knowing what you're supposed to do when working. New employees ask themselves: ''What is the purpose of the job? How does it fit into the system? What kind of power and influence does this position have. Am I doing the right things? How will I know when I'm doing a good job?''

Job candidates ask themselves the same questions, yet few firms are readily able to provide a job description upon request.

ROLE OF JOB AUDITS AND DESCRIPTIONS (Continued)

Job searchers know the adage, ''If you don't know where you're going, you'll probably end up somewhere else.'' An equally appropriate maxim for employers is ''If you don't know what you're looking for, you won't know what you've got.'' That's a scary thought in these times of high turnover and competition for applicants.

Organizations that have developed clear expectations are able to define, on paper, what an individual should be able to accomplish. Since maintaining clear communication is the big obstacle facing business today, job descriptions provide the candidate, and later the employee, with a focus for job performance.

Job descriptions should not be carved in stone. They should evolve with the changing needs of the organization and be reviewed before each new person fills the position. There is no expectation that job descriptions will be followed to the letter, but they provide a bench mark from which to start.

Job descriptions also hold managers and employees accountable. In the hustle and bustle of business, it is easy to get so absorbed in certain tasks that other responsibilities are neglected. While job descriptions should not be used as weapons for keeping employees in line, they can be used as reminders of specific roles and responsibilities.

If you already have job descriptions, now may be a good time to review them for accuracy. Compare the tasks outlined with the actual duties being performed. Ask persons in the job what they would change.

CONDUCTING A JOB AUDIT

Begin a job audit by looking at the actual job in relation to the entire organization. Does it serve a valuable role? Do the duties overlap those of other positions? Is this okay? Can parts of this job be eliminated or automated?

Consult with other managers for their input. Ask them for insight on how the job could be better defined or improved.

Here are four questions you might ask an employee in the position being audited:

☐ What duties listed in the job description are you no longer performing?

☐ What tasks do you perform that are not listed on the job description?

☐ What suggestions do you have for improving this job?

☐ What tasks do you think should be eliminated from this job?

People already working in these positions may have certain biases, so it is important to interview them rather than ask them to complete the form. Do not attempt to conduct the audit without the job holder. No one is closer to the job.

If you are creating a new position, it is important to look before you leap. Is this new job really needed or is the pile of work simply a result of a seasonal rush?

CONDUCTING A JOB AUDIT (Continued)

Figure 3—Do you need the job checklist

DO YOU NEED THE JOB?
Ask these questions before creating a new position

1. What is the purpose of this new job?
2. Who is presently performing these tasks?
3. How long have the employees who presently perform this task been overloaded?
4. Is this added business the result of a cycle or is the pace more permanent?
5. What will be the initial goals of this position and how long will it take to accomplish them?
6. What is the best that can happen if we fill this position with a good person?
7. Is there enough work for a full-time position? Can it be performed by a part-time employee?
8. Can some of the overload duties be switched to another area within the same department or location?
9. Is this a true need or can the systems in this function be streamlined for better productivity?
10. How much will this new position cost?
11. Is there sufficient labor market to choose from?
12. Will this position exist 24 months from now?
13. Have you checked with all other parties involved to determine if everyone feels there is a need?
14. How will other departments view adding this position? (They may feel their need is just as important.)
15. What impact will the creation of this new position have on the jobs from which the tasks are being removed?
16. What is the worst that can happen if we don't create this position?

Figure 3 provides a list of questions to ask before creating and filling a new position. Take care to examine the justification for the new position. It's a long term commitment.

Figure 4—Sample job audit form

JOB AUDIT FORM

Job Title _____   Dept. _____

Audit conducted by _____   Date _____

Duties
Major:

Minor:

Relationships (including number of employees supervised)

Training required

Education/Licenses/Certifications

Experience required (Identify specific skills.)

Physical requirements

On the job hazards/working conditions

Source of audit information_____

CONDUCTING A JOB AUDIT (Continued)

A sample job audit is provided in Figure 4, on preceding page.

Have someone other than the jobholder complete the audit. As we stated before, jobholders sometimes have a distorted view of what they do and how much time it takes. With another person asking the questions, the answers will be more realistic. If more than one person holds this position, interview all of them and take an average of the responses.

Figure 5—List of job audit questions

QUESTIONS TO ASK DURING A JOB AUDIT

- What duties does the person perform? (Be specific in description.)
- What tools, services and/or accommodations does a person need to complete these duties?
- Who supervises the person in this position?
- With which other people does this person interact, both in and out of the company?
- Is the person performing the job able to complete all duties in the time allotted?
- What formal training does a person need to perform this job, if any?
- What skills does this person need to complete this job? (Include technical, interpersonal, organizational and problem solving skills.)
- How is the person performing this job evaluated?

When completing the audit form, be as specific as possible. Describing a duty as ''Takes care of all the inventory paperwork,'' isn't very clear. A better way to describe this duty is: ''Responsible for the completion of all paperwork on incoming inventory. This includes, but is not limited to, checking manifests against actual counts, recording and assigning storage for all incoming freight, maintaining accurate control over all internal distribution of inventory. This responsibility entails 60 percent of average weekly time.'' While the second description is more involved, it is also more accurate and gives a realistic picture of what the job entails.

In addition to interviewing the jobholders, examine the job's overall role in the organization. Look at factors like role influence, contact with customers, career pathing to other positions and relation to other functions within the same department. The more information gathered, the more complete the job description will be.

Figure 6—Sample job audit form

JOB AUDIT FORM

Job Title _Delivery Van Driver_   Dept. _Transportation_

Audit conducted by _Bob Elliott_   Date _7/19/90_

Duties

Major: _Deliver packages to local customers. Sort packages for delivery. Daily truck operational inspection. Maintain good customer relations. Operate safely at all times. Complete all delivery paperwork._

Minor: _Maintain truck. Clean truck on daily basis (interior once a day, exterior twice a week.) Maintain updates safety regulations in truck._

Relationships (including number of employees supervised)

Reports to transportation manager. Supervises no one. Occasionally trains new drivers.

Training required

Training to drive step vans or similar vehicle. Ability to understand manifests and safety rules and traffic laws.

Education/Licenses/Certifications _Valid chauffer's license for this state._

Experience required (Identify specific skills.)

3 years experience driving step vans or similar vehicle. Very familiar with local streets. Ability to deal with customers in a positive manner.

Physical requirements

Must be able to drive truck with manual brakes and steering. Lift up to 70 lbs.

On the job hazards/working conditions _Normal hazards associated with driving a truck in local traffic. Potential lifting injuries._

Source of audit information _Interview with 4 drivers._

BUILDING A JOB DESCRIPTION

Once an audit has been completed, the job description can be written with ease. A job description is divided into the following parts: job summary, major duties, minor duties, relationships, qualifications and compensation.

The job summary is a brief, 2-3 sentence overview of the position as illustrated on page 11. Major and minor duties consist of those functions delineated in the job audit. Major duties are those of primary concern that generally consume the majority of time. Minor duties are those that play a secondary role in how the job is performed. Relationships cover the reporting structure, to whom the position reports and who, if anyone, reports to that position.

Describe what needs to be done, not what is being done presently. The present jobholder may be going above and beyond assigned duties. In this area, also include how the person filling this position will be evaluated.

Qualifications cover necessary skills, experience and education. Be careful to list only those qualifications that are necessary. Requiring a college degree, for instance, may not reflect what is actually necessary and may be construed as discriminatory. Necessary training is also included in this section.

Structure of compensation, such as commissions, hourly work and eligibility for overtime, can be listed on the job description. The actual rates should not be listed since they will probably change more often than the description. Figure 7 on page 15 provides a list of factors to consider in the structuring of compensation.

After the description has been developed, have it reviewed by those in the position for inaccuracies or omissions.

Job descriptions should be reviewed at least once per year. This task should not be complicated unless there have been significant changes in the organization.

Using Job Descriptions in the Selection Process

A job description helps the applicant understand the position and its role in the organization.

Show the job description to each finalist. Make sure these individuals fully understand the job requirements. Give each an opportunity to fully examine it and ask questions. Rushing a person through this process defeats its purpose.

If you want to hire someone who does not quite fit the job description, don't be afraid to modify the job to fit the applicant. Now that you have a grasp of the positions you want to fill, it is time to examine the laws and statutes covering the hiring process.

Figure 7—Sample compensation profile form

		COMPENSATION PROFILE FORM		
Type of Compensation	Present Policy	Competitor's Policy	How We Compare	Recommendations
Wages				
Salary increases				
Bonuses				
Profit Sharing				
Flexible hours				
Paid vacation				
Paid holidays				
Paid sick leave				
Paid disability				

Other paid leave
    Jury duty
    Funeral
    Military
    Marriage
    Pregnancy				

Health insurance				
Dental insurance				
Disability insurance				
Life insurance				
Pension plan				
Savings plan				
Credit union				
Education benefits				
Child benefits				
Elder care				
Other				

BUILDING A JOB DESCRIPTION (Continued)

Figure 8—Sample job description

SAMPLE JOB DESCRIPTION

Job Title: Purchasing Manager

Job Summary: Coordinates and approves all purchasing activities including the bidding process and office supplies budgeting.

Major duties: Coordinates overall purchasing effort for all corporate purchases of more than $100. Supervises bidding process on all corporate purchases of $500 or more. Serves as a purchasing resource for department managers and executives. Responsible for the accounting of all purchasing. Supervises purchasing staff.

Minor duties: Hires and trains all purchasing staff. Serves on corporate planning council. Maintains up-to-date catalogs and resources for purchasing needs. Prepares annual budget for purchasing department. Maintains relations with vendors as necessary.

Relationships: Reports to vice-president for operations. Supervises two purchasing specialists and one secretary.

Qualifications: Solid working knowledge of the purchasing process with a minimum of two years direct experience in purchasing and supervision of others. Substantial knowledge of budgeting including staffing costs. Excellent written, verbal and negotiating skills.

Compensation: Commensurate with experience. Check current compensation charts for actual salary and benefits package.

Descriptions prepared by _____ Date _____

Figure 9—Sample job description

SAMPLE JOB DESCRIPTION

Job Title: Receptionist

Job Summary: Serves as receptionist for an office of 20 along with minor clerical and secretarial duties.

Major duties: Answers phones for an office of 20 with 23 inbound lines. Takes and distributes messages. Performs minor research tasks for office manager as requested.

Minor duties: Minor typing and filing duties. Mail sorting and distribution. Maintains coffee/break room and purchases essential supplies.

Relationships: Reports to office manager. Supervises no one.

Qualifications: Six months PBX experience. Typing 40 words per minute. Excellent verbal and written communication skills.

Compensation: Commensurate with experience. Check current compensation charts for actual salary and benefits package.

Description prepared by _____ Date _____

THE LEGAL SIDE OF HIRING

PHILOSOPHICAL VS. PRACTICAL

In this litigious society, the laws regulating the selection of employees have become of crucial concern. These laws have been written to protect applicants and employees, and can be of considerable cost to employers if not followed. For the purposes of hiring, a working knowledge of federal, state and local legislation is essential.

The philosophical reasons for the enactment of these laws have been to prevent discrimination and unjust treatment of employees or applicants. One must be careful, however, to note that they apply only to the protected classes identified. White males under forty years of age, for example are, as a class, not protected. If a person of this class is a Vietnam veteran, however, he might be protected under the Rehabilitation Act of 1973, but only if he is applying to an organization under the Act's jurisdiction.

This is just one example of the complexities surrounding the employment process, with new cases and variations being decided every day. The best rule of thumb is to look at every applicant with an unbiased eye. If an action looks discriminatory, it most likely is.

Having a company policy that renounces discrimination is not enough. If the company rejects discrimination on paper, but maintains an all-white management in a predominantly black community, for instance, it is in violation of Title VII of the Civil Rights Act of 1964.

With over 400 federal laws pertaining to employee rights and selection, it would be counterproductive to discuss each one. Therefore, only the major laws and applications will be covered.

FEDERAL LEGISLATION

The Civil Rights Act of 1964 is the cornerstone to anti-discrimination legislation in the United States. Title VII of this act covers labor and employment. It provides for the removal of artificial, arbitrary and unnecessary barriers to employment when these barriers discriminate against individuals on the basis of race, sex, marital status or religious beliefs.

Title VII was amended in 1978 to include the **Pregnancy Discrimination Act** which prohibits discrimination on the basis of childbirth, pregnancy or related medical conditions.

The Age Discrimination in Employment Act, also amended in 1978, prohibits employers from discriminating in the hiring of individuals 40 years of age and older.

The Rehabilitation Act of 1973 was enacted to prohibit discrimination against otherwise qualified handicapped individuals. This act only applies to employers holding federal contracts in excess of $2500 or who receive financial assistance from the federal government.

The Immigration Reform and Control Act prohibits employers from hiring illegal aliens. It requires all new hires to produce specified documents proving they are legally eligible to work in the United States.

The Fair Labor Standards Act, as amended by the **Equal Pay Act**, sets minimum wages as well as overtime and equal pay standards.

Use of the polygraph and voice print devices is prohibited by the **Polygraph Protection Act** enacted in 1988.

Figure 10—Federal employment legislation chart

FEDERAL EMPLOYMENT LEGISLATION
Civil Rights Act (1964) (Title VII)
Rehabilitation Act (1973)
Pregnancy Discrimination Act (1978)
Age Discrimination in Employment Act (1978)
Fair Labor Standards Act (1938)
Equal Pay Act (1964)
Immigration Reform and Control Act (1986)
Employee Polygraph Protection Act (1988)

WHO IS AFFECTED?

Private employers, state and local governments, educational institutions and labor organizations having 15 or more employees are covered by Title VII. Employees in these organizations have to have been employed each working day in each of 20 or more calendar weeks in the current or preceding calendar year. The Pregnancy Discrimination Act of 1978 and the Age Discrimination in Employment Act cover the same parameters.

The Immigration Reform and Control Act (IRCA) is the exception to these guidelines. This legislation requires all newly hired employees show proof of their eligibility to work within three days of beginning employment. IRCA includes all employers, regardless of size. This means, for example, that the part-time housekeeper you hire must show proof of eligibility to work in the United States.

The **Equal Employment Opportunity Commission (EEOC)** is charged with enforcing Title VII, the Pregnancy Discrimination Act, the Age Discrimination in Employment Act and the Equal Pay Act. It accomplishes this task through district offices throughout the United States.

The Rehabilitation Act of 1973 is enforced by the Office of Federal Contract Compliance Programs and each federal agency.

To assist employers in understanding the federal legislation covering employee selection, the EEOC issued the **Uniform Guidelines for Employee Selection Procedures** in 1978. The questions asked by an employer cannot be deemed unlawful. What the employer does with the answers can be called into question.

An interviewer might ask, for example, ''That's quite an accent you've got. Where does it come from?'' While the actual intent may be innocent, the interviewer's question could be interpreted as a judgment that this person should not be hired due to his or her heritage. Every interview question must have a business necessity. If the position being filled is one involving significant customer contact, for example, a question regarding the accent might be acceptable if it impairs the person's ability to communicate in English. The more appropriate tactic in this instance would be to engage that person in a discussion about customer service to determine how well the applicant communicates.

There are a few instances where an employer can set a standard restricting the employment of a certain group. These requirements are called **Bona Fide Occupational Qualifications (BFOQ),** and are based on business necessity.

A typical example would be restricting men from serving in certain areas of a health club that are private to female patrons. Since BFOQ's are so severely limited, the best policy is to assume there are no exceptions. Apply each hiring requirement as if all applicants are eligible.

AFFIRMATIVE ACTION

Affirmative action is the action taken by an employer to ensure equal opportunity for all protected groups. Affirmative action programs detail the ways in which this commitment is carried out. While not all employers are required to have a formal program, these policies are developed for one of three reasons:

1. As a voluntary commitment to equal opportunity

2. As mandated by federal law (Executive Order 11246 requires all federal contractors and subcontractors and recipients of federal funds of $50,000 or more to develop and implement a written affirmative action program monitored by the Department of Labor.)

3. As required, because of discriminatory practices and/or impacts on protected classes.

An affirmative action program includes the following objectives:

- Establishing a company policy and commitment to equal opportunity

- Identifying positions in the company where those in protected classes are under-utilized

- Setting specific, measurable and attainable goals for hiring and promotion within each area of the company, with target dates for completion

- Reviewing all hiring criteria to be sure they are legitimate requirements of the job

- Making concerted efforts to locate qualified persons in protected classes who meet job requirements or who can be trained to do so

- Informing all managers and supervisors that they are accountable for helping to achieve the objectives of the affirmative action program

- Assigning one top company official the responsibility and authority for the program and its progress

Figure 11—Key components of affirmative action

KEY COMPONENTS OF AFFIRMATIVE ACTION

- Employer is not required to establish an affirmative action program unless it has shown discrimination in the past. (The exception is contractors having $50,000 in federal·contracts and more than 50 employees.)

- There must be a clear assignment of who will direct the program. (A senior executive is usually required to fill this role.)

- The plan must have clearly stated procedures.

- The plan must contain a clearly stated equal opportunity policy.

- The plan must contain specific goals and timetables for hiring from protected groups who are under-represented.

Once an affirmative action program is in place, it is the organization's responsibility to actively recruit members of protected classes for present and future openings. This recruitment is accomplished in a variety of ways:

- Establishing relations with nearby colleges and job services to keep them informed of your staffing needs

- Attending job fairs sponsored in the local area

- Placing advertisements in periodicals that attract large numbers of women and minorities

- Using female and minority recruiters

- Using photographs of women and minorities in advertisements

- Holding informational tours of the company for specified groups

Merely having the appropriate number of protected class employees in your firm does not accomplish affirmative action. These individuals must be qualified for the positions they hold. If they are not, training arrangements should be made to qualify them if other suitable candidates cannot be found. Examining agencies scrutinize an organization's practices, not just the end results.

Establishing and completing an affirmative action program is a complex task requiring commitment from the entire organization. For additional information, qualified experts should be consulted.

EMPLOYMENT ISSUES

The key element in deciding whether a particular requirement can be considered a hiring condition is whether the requirement is related to or required by the job. While some requirements can be clearly identified as discriminatory, others have an impact on certain protected classes but are not obviously discriminatory. The more common job requirements are listed below with their allowability. Check your hiring policies to see if you might be violating any of these standards:

☐ **Age requirements:** Under the Age Discrimination in Employment Act as amended in 1978, employers may not discriminate on the basis of age except in situations where there is a bona fide occupational qualification.

☐ **Employment of aliens:** Aliens must have permission to work in the United States. Employers are responsible for checking employees' status for their eligibility to work within three days of hire.

☐ **Alienage:** An employer cannot require citizenship as a standard for hire under Title VII of the Civil Rights Act of 1964. The exceptions to this rule usually revolve around national security.

☐ **Appearance and dress:** Applicants cannot be rejected on the basis of appearance and dress if the appearance and dress is typical of their culture. Employers can set dress standards if there is a business necessity such as safety requirements.

☐ **Arrest and criminal records:** Arrest records cannot be used as a basis for rejecting an applicant. Employers are prohibited from rejecting an applicant on the basis of a conviction, unless that conviction is substantially related to job responsibilities. An applicant who has been convicted of shoplifting, for instance, can be refused a job as a security guard.

☐ **Blacklisting:** Most states prohibit blacklisting of applicants for any reason.

☐ **Credit requirement:** Employers may not require an acceptable credit rating as a condition for employment unless they can demonstrate business necessity. An example of business necessity would be the hiring of a cashier or financial manager.

☐ **Dependent's status:** An employer cannot reject a female candidate because she has children of pre-school age, when no such requirement exists for male applicants. Nor can she be refused employment because she is a single parent, since this factor is not related to business necessity.

☐ **Education:** Employers may require a certain level or type of education as a requirement only if it can be demonstrated to be a business necessity. A high school diploma can be required, for example, if the employer can demonstrate that the skills learned in high school are substantially necessary to perform the job.

☐ **Fingerprinting:** Fingerprinting of applicants is generally accepted in all states except New York, where there are some limitations.

☐ **Hair requirement:** Employers may not have a hair requirement that differs from men to women.

☐ **Handicap:** Employers subject to the Rehabilitation Act of 1973 are required to provide reasonable accommodation to handicapped applicants. This compliance may include wheelchair access, special aids for telephones, and special furniture.

☐ **Health requirements:** If an applicant fails a physical examination, the employer may refuse employment, provided that the requirements in the exam demonstrate that the applicant would not be able to perform the job.

☐ **Height/weight requirement:** An employer can require a certain height or weight standard if it can be demonstrated to be a business necessity. Requiring flight attendants to meet a height requirement for example, has been found to be a business necessity because of safety considerations.

☐ **Language requirement:** If an employer can demonstrate that speaking English is a business necessity for a particular job, then proficiency in English may be required. A typical example in this case would be that of a retail clerk or telephone operator.

☐ **Marital status:** An employer may not have a policy prohibiting the employment of married women, unless the same policy applies to married men.

☐ **Military record:** Applicants may not be rejected on the basis of having a less-than-honorable military discharge, unless the employer can demonstrate the decision was related to job performance.

☐ **National origin:** An applicant may not be rejected because of national origin, unless the employer can demonstrate a bona fide occupational qualification.

☐ **Nepotism:** Prohibiting nepotism may be in violation of Title VII if it results in discriminatory impact on one or more protected classes. For example, if the major employer in a small town with a large minority population prohibits the hiring of employees' relatives, this may result in disparate impact.

EMPLOYMENT ISSUES (Continued)

☐ **Polygraph/lie detector:** Private sector employers are prohibited from using polygraphs, voice print devices and other related technology in the selection of employees. Major exceptions to this law are certain defense, security and pharmaceutically related jobs.

☐ **Pregnancy:** An employer may not discriminate against women affected by pregnancy, childbirth and other related medical conditions.

☐ **Recruitment:** There are no specific prohibitions regarding the recruitment of employees. An employer who grants preferential treatment to friends, relatives or employee referrals, for example, may be in violation of Title VII, if protected classes are under-represented in the firm.

☐ **Religious conviction:** Reasonable accommodation must be made for an applicant's religious convictions, and the employer may not reject the applicant on that basis, unless it would cause undue hardship. An applicant, for example, who asks that an interview be moved because of the observance of a religious holiday should not suffer in the selection process because of this request.

☐ **Sexual status:** Males or females may not be precluded from a position unless the employer has a bona fide occupational qualification. Men, for example, may be restricted from female locker room jobs.

☐ **No-spouse requirement:** An employer may prohibit the hiring of a spouse providing the rule is neutral. In other words, if the wife of a male employee cannot be hired, the husband of a female employee cannot be hired.

☐ **Strength requirement:** Provided the requirement is a business necessity, an employer can ask applicants to pass a strength test. An auto mechanic's position might have this requirement if the employer can demonstrate its legitimacy.

☐ **Testing (aptitude/psychological):** Employers may not require applicants to submit to aptitude or psychological testing unless they can demonstrate relatedness to job performance. Tests must be validated and be approved by the EEOC. They must not have an unequal impact on protected classes.

☐ **Testing (drugs):** There are no specific laws prohibiting drug testing at present. Issues around invasion of privacy, discriminatory impact and accuracy are still being debated. It is best to have a well-defined policy in place before testing is initiated.

☐ **Work experience:** Applicants may be required to have particular work experiences and skills, provided the employer can demonstrate business necessity. The amount of experience must be reasonable. Requiring a security guard to have five years' experience is unreasonable.

Figure 12—Summary of positions data

		Approved Salary Range			Actual Salary Range			Average Empl. Age	Average Years Service	% minority	% female
Position Title	Staffing Level	Min.	Avg.	Max.	Min.	Avg.	Max.				

SUMMARY OF POSITIONS DATA

STATE AND LOCAL LEGISLATION

The scope of state laws are generally more comprehensive and more restrictive than federal statutes. Employers must comply with all federal, state and local laws affecting their local.

If you are unfamiliar with them, become acquainted with the state laws affecting hiring. While there is no federal legislation regarding Acquired Immune Deficiency Syndrome (AIDS), for example, a number of large cities now have anti-discrimination laws covering those afflicted.

Most state anti-discrimination legislation takes affect with three or more employees. Title VII, however, does not affect an employer with fewer than fifteen.

Examine all parts of the hiring process. This effort includes applications, interviews, record keeping and job postings. Be sure your procedures fall within local guidelines.

State procedures parallel federal anti-discrimination laws. All complaints must be filed with the Equal Employment Opportunity Commission (EEOC) along with the state agency. EEOC, however, defers its investigation for 60 days. If the state chooses to investigate, the EEOC will await the outcome before deciding to act.

States and municipalities vary significantly in their legislation and enforcement. Be sure you are aware of your organization's obligations.

REACHING OUT FOR APPLICANTS

DEVELOPING A RECRUITING POLICY

Do you have the applicants you need when you need them? Labor sources throughout the United States are changing drastically. The overall population is aging. The Baby Boom is over, and labor-force growth will come primarily from what were once considered minority races.

How well-prepared is your organization for these changes? What differences have you seen in recent applicants? Your ability to anticipate and react to changes in the work force ensures successful recruiting. But how can this be accomplished?

You can begin by developing a clearly-defined recruiting philosophy. Determine what qualities are needed in every employee so you can draw a picture of the right recruit. In addition, the company should have clearly defined recruiting goals and a means for communicating these goals to all employees.

Picturing the Right Recruit

With the wide variety of people who apply to your company, it is difficult to determine who will best fit into open positions. By developing a clear profile of people who succeed in your company, you will be better able to select from those who complete applications.

While the desired skills may vary, successful candidates must share the same general values of current employees. Look around your organization and take stock of the present work force. What kind of work style do they have? Is it fast-paced? Are they more deliberate? Are they jovial or are they a solemn group?

What about the work place itself? Is it noisy? Can people concentrate? What kind of expectations does management have concerning performance and individual contribution? These, and a host of other factors all need to be considered. This composite picture will provide you with a guide for identifying compatible applicants.

DEVELOPING A RECRUITING POLICY
(Continued)

Predicting your goals for recruiting enables you to develop the sources you need for the future. If a particular area experiences higher turnover or greater expansion, promoting these openings on an informal basis, in advance, eases the task when the actual need arises.

Review past hiring patterns. Are there certain times of the year when the company experiences more turnover? Do employees with certain backgrounds or experiences appear to be the ones that always leave? These might be the type of individuals to avoid recruiting. Have employees with particular skills or experience succeeded better than the average? These are individuals you want to pursue. Noting these patterns will enhance your recruiting efforts.

Once these goals have been established, they must be communicated to everyone in the organization. Since some of the most reliable employees will come from internal referrals, it is imperative that all employees know about openings you are seeking to fill.

LOCATING INTERNAL CANDIDATES

Internal candidates and applicants referred by current employees are the most cost-efficient way of filling vacancies. With the promotion of a current employee you get a person who already knows the organization. It also proves to other employees that there is opportunity for moving up.

Applicants referred by employees will probably be more reliable since the reputation of the employee referring is at stake. Once again you save recruiting dollars on advertising.

When making promotions and encouraging referrals, you should clearly explain how people will be considered. Those who are referred will not be automatically hired.

If an employee is considered for promotion into an open position, that person must understand there is no guarantee. Such misunderstandings can result in hard feelings and damaged employee morale.

The best way to handle referrals and promotions is to develop a plan of action.

- Make sure communication regarding all openings is clear to all employees. This eliminates rumors and misunderstandings.

- Design a workable referral and promotion system. Consider how long vacancies should be posted to give employees a chance to respond. Make sure everyone involved knows how the system works. Set standards that are fair to all. Avoid any appearance of favoritism.

- If you are considering someone for a position in another department, notify the employee's current supervisor of the possible move. The supervisor might be able to shed some additional light on the person's performance. Besides, proper protocol requires that the current boss be informed. "Stealing" employees creates animosity.

- Be open to candidates with a different background than you might normally consider. If they match the qualifications but not the picture in your head, enlarge your picture. They may have some excellent qualities you hadn't considered.

LOCATING INTERNAL CANDIDATES
(Continued)

- Record the names of people who make referrals and the people they referred. If some have a better track record than others, go back to them with vacancies. If certain people suggest people who are poor matches, you will probably want to avoid them.

- Reward those who make good referrals. This not only encourages them to continue but encourages others as well.

- Set internal promotion goals. Decide how many positions you would like to fill internally each year, then encourage internal applications. If employees see there really is a chance to move up, you will see a resulting increase in productivity.

ORGANIZING AN EXTERNAL RECRUITING PLAN

When you choose to recruit externally, there are a number of factors to be considered. Even the simple task of placing a classified ad has become more complex.

Applicants can be recruited through a variety of sources. Which sources you should use depend on the position being filled.

These sources can be divided into seven categories:

- Recruitment advertising agencies
- Recruiting services
- College placement centers
- Public job services
- Professional association data bases
- Conferences and career fairs
- Newspaper advertising

Before deciding on which sources to use, review the profile of the position you seek to fill. From what categories of people would likely candidates come? If you are hiring counter help for instance, newspaper advertisements, college placement centers and public job services are probably your best bet. On the other hand, locating managers with technical experience can best be accomplished by networking through recruiting services, professional organizations and by announcing the opening in trade journals. The more clearly defined your candidate profile, the better you can target possible applicants. This saves both time and expense.

ORGANIZING AN EXTERNAL RECRUITING PLAN (Continued)

Figure 13—Cost of a new management hire

MEMORANDUM

TO: Jack Clark, Vice President Production
FROM: Ralph Needick, Operations

Here is the final breakdown on replacing Sue Green, our manager of distribution.

Cash Expenses

Classified advertising (3 display ads for one week.)	$ 975
Postage, phone, copying, miscellaneous	75

Labor @ V.P.'s and managers' time (average $37/hour)

Search planning meetings (5 hours)	185
Development & placement of ads (2 hours)	74
Review of applications (2 hours)	74
Phone interviews (16 hours)	592
Second interviews (8 hours)	296
Decision making (3 hours)	111
Negotiation (5 hours)	185
Orientation and planning (10 hours)	370
Training (40 hours over 3 months)	1480
Miscellaneous administration (5 hours)	185

Staff time (average $12/hour)

Administration of search (30 hours)	360
Secretarial support (20 hours)	240
Orientation and training support (10 hours)	120
GRAND TOTAL	$5322

Note: This does not include unproductive training time on the new hire's part!

RECRUITING SOURCES

Below are brief descriptions of these recruiting sources:

Recruitment Advertising Agencies

Recruitment advertising agencies are used by many large companies to attract great numbers of applicants. They assist by designing attractive advertisements and helping with media placement. Since they concentrate solely on the area of recruitment advertising, they know what strategies work.

Hiring one of these agencies is not generally an expensive process, since they receive their commissions from the publications in which they place advertisements. When selecting an agency, consider the following:

- How large is the agency? Do they have several offices? If your company has a number of sites, can any of these offices be used?

- What do their references say about their performance? Do they seem to handle some industries better than others?

- How much lead time does the agency need to prepare your campaign?

- How aggressive is the agency? In tighter labor markets, more creative techniques will have to be used. Can they demonstrate a successful track record in this area?

- What services will be charged for, and what is included in the package? Will they charge extra for tracking ad placement for instance?

- Does the agency insist on a contract? If yes, negotiate a trial period.

Recruiting Services

Recruiting Services vary widely in their approach and quality. They can be separated into four categories: employment agencies, temporary agencies, executive recruiters and executive search firms (also called headhunters).

EMPLOYMENT AGENCIES

Employment agencies provide companies with applicants for clerical and staff positions. Their fees may be charged to the employee, the employer, or both. A good agency can provide you with quality candidates, saving you time and money. But be sure to check references before making a selection.

RECRUITING SOURCES (Continued)

TEMPORARY AGENCIES

Temporary agencies provide employers with help on an ''as needed'' basis. This help may consist of everything from clerical and staff support to highly trained individuals such as accountants and technical managers. The employer pays the agency and the agency in turn pays the temporary employee. Most exact a penalty if the employee decides to take a full-time position with the employer. As with any agency, it is best to check references or obtain referrals.

Figure 14—Selecting a temporary service

SELECTING A TEMPORARY SERVICE

Find out if the service:

Is a member of the National Association of Temporary Services?

Adheres to NATS' code of ethics?

Has a formal policy on evaluating each temporary's assignment?

Provides instruction on office equipment?

Provides references from other clients?

Checks references and background on the people it provides?

Has a professional staff that develops client relationships so they know your needs?

Has a formal contract you can take away and have reviewed by an attorney?

EXECUTIVE RECRUITERS

Executive recruiters attempt to match entry-level up through middle management job seekers with appropriate openings. They work on either a retainer or contingency basis and can receive the equivalent of as much as 30 percent of the successful candidate's first year salary. In other words, you as the employer would have to pay the employee's compensation, plus 30 percent to the agency.

It is best to compare these costs to what it would cost you to conduct the search yourself. As always, thoroughly check the references before proceeding.

PROFESSIONAL/EXECUTIVE SEARCH FIRMS (HEADHUNTERS)

Professional/executive search firms (headhunters) work exclusively for client companies to fill senior level positions or needs for certain technical expertise. These firms begin by interviewing the client's executives and investigating its organization. They generally specialize in one industry.

The professionals targeted by these firms are usually working managers in the field who can be lured away by more challenging or lucrative offers. This type of service is generally reserved for acquiring senior level professionals. It is important to check references and perform a thorough interview before making a commitment.

College placement centers

College placement centers offer a wealth of candidates for companies of all sizes. Most centers now work with both newly graduating students and alumni. This means you obtain applicants with both experience and state-of-the-art training. Contact your local two-year and four-year colleges and ask about the placement candidates. Developing a relationship with center professionals will ensure that you get special attention when looking to fill positions. You may want to visit with faculty or be present at classes and career fairs. Faculty have a great deal of influence over students and can steer the best ones in your direction.

In addition to filling full-time positions, college placement centers can also be a good source of part-time help or interns. Not only will you find the personnel you need to get the work done, you may also find a number of excellent candidates for full-time positions.

RECRUITING SOURCES (Continued)

Public Job Services

Public job services can also be found in your locale. Supported through federal, state or local funding, these agencies maintain lists of candidates from a wide variety of sources. To get the most from a job service, develop a relationship with the counselors or coordinators of these agencies. Let them get to know your company and the types of people you generally seek.

Professional associations

Professional associations maintain large data bases of members and others working in the industry. By contacting the ones in your field, you may be able to tap into a wealth of applicants. In some cases, these associations offer a computer matching service to serve employer and applicant members.

Conferences and career fairs

Conferences and career fairs offer a wonderful opportunity to discover new talent for now and the future. In certain industries, there has been an explosion in the number of career fairs. Take advantage of this chance to recruit new professionals.

Newspaper Advertising

Newspaper advertising has been the most common form of announcing a vacancy. As the labor market begins to tighten, advertising in newspapers will become less and less effective for filling many positions. With the specialization of many positions, companies will need to more actively recruit using media that attract specific populations.

CLASSIFIED ADS

Newspaper advertising should remain one of the best means for attracting workers in retail and hospitality (restaurants, hotels, etc.) and other industries where high turnover is common and somewhat unavoidable. Even in these situations the advertisements will have to be tailored to specific populations. Two advertisements for example, one aimed at teenagers and another at seniors, will work better than one generally worded ad. These groups respond to different attitudes, jargon and job benefits.

Before developing newspaper advertisements, review your local dailies. The largest readership is not as relevant a factor as who those readers are.

Look through the classifieds. Count the number of advertisements you see for jobs related to your openings. If there are too few, consider another paper or another medium.

Read the wording: What works? What doesn't? If you see the same ad over and over, you might conclude that the response is good. Examine why and then adapt those strategies to your advertisement.

DISPLAY ADS

Besides classifieds, you have the option of placing display advertisements. A quarter or half page ad obviously gives you more opportunity to sell the position. But most studies indicate that small space advertisements will draw 75-80 percent of the response of a full page ad for much less cost.

In addition to the local papers, there are also national and regional publications. As a general rule, however, these are not timely enough for the average opening.

WRITING A JOB NOTICE

Writing a job notice is similar to writing any advertisement. Readers must find the job attractive based on the description you provide. It should be an honest and accurate picture of what the employee has to do. Be careful not to mislead the reader into thinking the job is something it isn't.

After placing the ad, you may receive a number of applications that are not appropriate for the position. See if these applicants might fit into other openings in the company.

RECRUITING SOURCES CHECKPOINTS

Checkpoints to follow when writing a job notice.

- ☑ Begin the ad with a descriptive title. Make sure the title you use accurately reflects the job and is understandable to the reader.

- ☑ Include a brief job description highlighting the most attractive points. Give the reader a perspective on how the job fits into the organization.

- ☑ List necessary education and experience. Make sure it really is necessary. (Requiring five years experience for a cashier, for example, is not realistic and may be viewed as discriminatory in certain instances.)

- ☑ Ask for a salary history. This will help you screen out those who are under or over qualified.

- ☑ Sell the job benefits. Point out how the employee will benefit by working in this position.

- ☑ Avoid colorful, but useless, adjectives. ''Fast-paced'' describes the environment. ''Exciting'' does not.

- ☑ Talk to the readers instead of simply listing duties. Help them to understand how much you care about hiring the right person.

- ☑ Eliminate all unnecessary words and phrases. Get right to the point. Quick reading advertisements get read, yet avoid abbreviations.

- ☑ Place yourself in the reader's position. What questions would you have about this job? Try to answer those concerns in the ad.

- ☑ You may want to omit the identity of your company if you want to avoid a deluge of unwanted applications or the responsibility of answering every response.

- ☑ How you would like candidates to respond is up to you.

NOTE: You may choose for instance, to ask telemarketing or customer service applicants to call so you can get a feel for their ability to communicate over the phone.

RECRUITING SOURCES
CHECKPOINTS (Continued)

Figure 15—Sample classified advertising

SAMPLE CLASSIFIED ADVERTISING

We Need You!

Restaurant Personnel

Opening a new Mexican Restaurant in Southeast Denver. We're looking for high energy individuals who enjoy a challenge. Experience is not necessary. We offer a complete training program. Sign up early and get the best hours! Apply in person between 2-4 pm weekdays to Burrito Bob's. 2222 S. Hampden Ave.

Office Manager

Manufacturer of novelties and gifts seeking a well organized office manager for its distribution center. Two years experience managing others an absolute must. Word processing and electronic spreadsheet skills preferable. Distribution center experience a plus. Apply to:
You Name It Gifts and Novelities
14 Girard Place, Suite 13-214
Coral Gables, Florida 33407
646-4843

BUDGETING FOR RECRUITING

Hiring employees can become an expensive proposition if costs are not monitored carefully. With the tightening labor market, employers can expect expenses to continue to rise.

When attracting applicants to your openings, try innovative strategies for getting attention. Not all recruitment advertising has to cost money. Word-of-mouth is one of the most powerful tools available. Other mediums are discussed later in this chapter.

When budgeting for recruiting, do not forget to include the indirect costs such as phone calls, secretarial time and the interview time of line managers. In addition to these expenses, the new employee will have to be oriented and trained to perform the job.

Occasionally calculate your company's recruiting and turnover costs. Combined, these two can be staggering. A little extra emphasis on retention and employee motivation can go a long way toward reducing recruiting expenses.

RECRUITING MEDIA

There are a wide variety of ways to reach applicants, from the traditional to the outrageous. Here is a collection of ideas that have worked to attract substantial numbers of applicants. Keep in mind that different labor groups respond to different messages. Your job is to find the matches.

Airplane banners attract attention at large events or gatherings.

Billboards can be placed in strategic locations such as close to a competitor's site.

Bumper stickers get exposure whenever the car is on the road.

Career fairs are a great place to display your company to a wide or narrow audience, depending on the fair's target.

Cinema billboards get the attention of young workers and seniors.

Direct mail can be tailored to garner the attention of a large number of potential applicants in a specific locale or profession.

Door hangers are effective where the recruiting is geographically limited, such as a college campus or retirement complex.

Envelope stuffers can be used to reach your customers who may generate referrals since they already use your products.

Job fairs are usually aimed at specific groups such as engineers and are a good way to showcase your organization.

Kiosks offer the opportunity to advertise in high traffic areas. You can also purchase portable kiosks to increase your exposure.

Leaflets that are aggressively written with easy contact instructions will attract the attention of those on the run.

Magnetic signs can be attached to vehicles, walls, tables and can serve as a very portable recruiting tool.

Open houses give the public an opportunity to see how your organization works. Set up a table at the end of the tour to encourage applications.

MORE RECRUITING MEDIA
(Continued)

Point-of-sale materials, distributed in retail stores, are convenient ways to catch customers who might be interested in working for your company.

Posters with tear-off coupons make it easy for potential applicants to fill out a short form and send it in.

Presentations to local groups by any employee should include a pitch about working for the company.

Radio can be tailored to the audience. Besides commercials, companies can use public service announcements and appearances on talk shows.

Restaurant place mats announce to a captive audience that the establishment is hiring.

Table tents also can grab the attention of restaurant patrons.

Telemarketing can be extremely effective if the pitch is prepared and executed correctly. This is generally used to access targeted audiences.

Television, especially during late night and daytime hours, can be very effective at reaching out-of-work applicants.

Trade shows, while not geared toward recruiting, provide an excellent opportunity to reach individuals in a particular field.

Transit advertising accesses those commuters working in your vicinity. It demonstrates that they can reach your company without needing a car.

ENHANCING RECRUITING IMAGE

Before commencing with a recruiting program, you must examine how your company is perceived in the community. Your recruiting effort will yield little result if there are questions about the organization's integrity, how it treats its employees, or a host of other situations.

The best way to determine the company's image is to simply ask around. Conduct an informal survey by asking those in the community questions like:

"What have you heard about our organization?"

"Do you know what products we make? Do you use them?"

"Do you know anyone who works for our organization?"

"What are your impressions, based on what they have said?"

While not everything you hear may be pleasant, for the average citizen, those are the truths. In addition to finding out the public's perception, you may learn some new things about the organization you did not know. Someone may even suggest better ideas for reaching the applicants you want.

Here are some points to keep in mind when trying to enhance the organization's image:

Overall company public relations: Be sure that those serving in the company's public relations function are fully informed about recruiting efforts. Provide them with as much information as possible on hiring and training endeavors and how these relate to community outreach.

Recruiting literature: To impress applicants you must have top notch materials explaining the company and its opportunities. If the literature is confusing or poorly produced, this will reflect badly on your efforts.

Front-line reception of applicants: How are applicants treated when they make contact? Is the receptionist well informed about openings and procedures? Are candidates treated professionally? That first impression goes along way toward selling the job.

Handling of the selection process: Do candidates understand the process? Is it timely and kept on course? Are interviewers prepared? Do you make an effort to "sell" the top candidate? It's the little things that make or break a recruiting effort.

Employee turnover: What do former employees say about the organization? Those who talk about long hours, difficult supervisors or confusing priorities only serve to damage the company's image. This is a perfect reason to work for better retention.

EXECUTING THE RECRUITING PLAN

As you begin to develop a strategy for recruiting applicants, it will help to investigate the motivations of the groups you are pursuing. By tailoring the recruiting message to the target groups, you will receive a better response in less time with fewer dollars.

The most basic way to determine these motivations is to simply list what you think the group's motivations would be. This is especially easy if you are a member of that group.

Figure 16—Recruiting plan options

RECRUITING PLAN OPTIONS

MEMORANDUM

TO: Jackie Toon, Operations Manager
FROM: Alex Quick, Recruiting Coordinator
RE: Recruiting plan for shipping, distributing, and telemarketing

After consulting with all departments involved and doing some research on the local labor market, I've developed a plan to increase our number of applicants. Below are the strategies I plan to use along with the dollar cost and projections for how many applicants will be yielded over a period of one month. We should be doing this on consistent basis rather than in fits and starts.

	Dollar Cost	Projected applicants
Direct mail to selected customers	$ 300	15
Newspaper display ads	1500	75
Employee referral campaign	550	65
Local JTPA program	25	15
Signs on local transit	400	40
Morning radio spots	600	50
Posters at all 7 community colleges	100	70
Letters to churches and senior centers	50	100
Estimated totals	$3525	430

Estimated cost per applicant = $8.20

To develop more insight, ask employees who are in the target group for their input. Finally, you may go out and ask actual members of the group about their interests and attitudes along with ideas they have for reaching the group.

Here are some sample questions:

"What is the most important feature to you in a job?"

"What was your last job?" or "Where are you working now?"

"Why did you accept that job?"

"What did you like most about your last job?"

"What did you like least about your last job?"

"What is the most important feature you look for in a supervisor?"

"How did you find out about your last job?"

Once you have developed a feeling for applicant motivations, you are ready to put the recruiting effort together. Compare the information in the job description with the applicants' motivations to determine the target groups.

Figure 17—Applicant pool survey

APPLICANT POOL SURVEY

Ask these questions when surveying your applicant pools.

- What was your last job?
- How did you learn of your last job?
- Why did you accept that job?
- What did you like most about your last job?
- What did you like least about your last job?
- What do you look for in a supervisor?
- What is the most important feature to you in a job?
- Please rank the following from most to least important:

      —Distance to work
      —Hours
      —Job duties
      —Pay
      —Work environment

EXECUTING THE RECRUITING PLAN
(Continued)

Now you can decide on the best strategies for reaching these applicants. Appendix A contains 85 strategies that organizations have successfully used for attracting applicants. Combine this list with the mediums mentioned above and budget for the most effective campaign.

The key to any recruiting strategy is research and planning. Even if the opening being filled is a sudden vacancy, plans should be in place to access the appropriate groups. An ongoing effort to locate the best applicants is the secret to recruiting success.

REVIEWING RÉSUMÉS AND APPLICATIONS

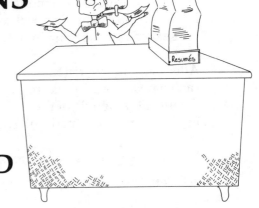

ROLES OF RÉSUMÉS AND APPLICATIONS

How effectively do you review résumés and applications? Are you getting the information you need to reach a clear decision?

While these documents are not the only factor in screening candidates, they are sometimes given too much emphasis in the hiring process. Résumés and applications must be viewed with skepticism. Studies show that as many as 30 percent of all applicants regularly exaggerate or misrepresent themselves on these documents. Even so, you can make the most of these submissions by following some simple guidelines.

Recognize the different roles résumés and applications play. While some companies use them interchangeably, résumés have traditionally been required for professional positions. Applications have been relegated to the areas of skilled and unskilled labor.

Résumés give applicants the opportunity to express themselves in what they consider the best light possible. You might compare résumés to newspaper advertisements. Both are selling a product, and how they are designed greatly influences the reader's opinion. Studies show that the average screener spends less than 45 seconds reviewing a résumé before deciding the fate of its owner.

Applications provide information in a more rigid form. Any gaps in information are immediately noticed. The information is easy to interpret since it is presented in the same order on each submission.

Before deciding on whether to ask for résumés or applications, consider criteria by which applicants will be screened. If you are looking for creative, self-reliant individuals, résumés will give you a better picture of their capacities. If you are hiring for assembly work, applicants' abilities to complete an application according to directions may be a deciding factor on whether to hire them.

REVIEWING A RÉSUMÉ

Determine your hiring criteria before you review a résumé. Simply looking for interesting facts and data will confuse the focus of who you should hire. List the optimal criteria, keeping in mind that you will not find the perfect candidate.

After determining criteria, you might want to create a checklist against which you can compare each applicant's qualifications. Make this a simple, easy-to-read document (a sample of this form is on the following page) that provides reliable information for comparison. You might even build-in a scoring system.

When reviewing résumés, break the examination into five categories:

- Overall appearance
- Organization
- Education/training
- Experience
- Other relevant activities

Overall appearance

The overall appearance of the résumé gives you an idea of how much care was taken in preparation, and the level of interest the applicant has in the job.

- Are there errors in spelling?
- Is proper grammar used?
- Is the printing readable?
- Is it printed on good quality paper (with an envelope to match)?
- Does it have a "textbook" appearance, as if the format was copied directly from a book?

Figure 18—Applicant screening form

APPLICANT SCREENING FORM

Position title _____ Date _____

Screener _____

Rate each applicant's résumé/application on the characteristics below
according to the following scales:

1=Does not meet expectations, 2=Meets expectations,
3=Exceeds expectations, 4=Outstanding

When you have rated all applicants decide on a cut-off according to your
hiring goals.

Applicant								Total

REVIEWING THE RÉSUMÉ
(Continued)

Organization

- Does the résumé provide the information you need?

- Is it apparent that the applicant included the data most critical to helping you decide? (In other words, is this person anticipating your needs?)

- Does it provide a clear path to the information, or is there no rhyme or reason?

- Can you understand the individual entries?

- Do you find the information you need when looking under the logical category?

A well-organized résumé probably means the applicant is well-organized on the job. You may also assume that this person can communicate adequately in other situations.

Education

When reviewing education qualifications, keep in mind that only relevant education may be considered. You cannot, for example, refuse employment to management applicants simply because they do not have college degrees. If you did, you would have to demonstrate how those applicants would not able to handle the job solely for that reason. Instead, you need to establish a level of experience comparable to a degree and evaluate on that basis.

In addition to reviewing for necessary qualifications, examine the motivations of someone with too much education for the position. Is this applicant truly interested in the position or just using it as a weigh station before moving on? If you do pass this person on, that question needs to be answered in the interview.

Be flexible with college majors. While applicants may not have completed the exact course work akin to job requirements, this does not mean they can't perform the job. For instance, an English major might perform very well in a management role. Technical applications may require certain courses of study, but flexibility in accepting a variety of majors and educational backgrounds broadens your field of applicants.

Remember to check all educational credentials with the granting institution. Unfortunately, some applicants fabricate their education as needed.

Experience

In many cases, an applicant's experience may be critical to whether that person can do the job. Be careful, however, of excluding candidates because they do not match the exact experience requirements. Hiring a person who fully meets the job's qualifications may be counterproductive, since that person can be bored with no new challenges.

When you review the experience section of a résumé, consider the following:

- Does the applicant list duties versus responsibilities? (What was actually done?)

- Is there a list of accomplishments? It's easy to do some jobs without really contributing. How do you know this person made a difference?

- How long did the applicant hold each position? If a person is moving progressively upward in a short time, that is commendable. It can also spell impatience and disloyalty. The applicant might also be unable to hold a job and is "dressing up" later job titles. Be careful to verify facts.

  If the person has held the same job for a number of years it can suggest stability or loyalty. On the other hand, it may suggest being too set in one's ways.

- Are the job titles authentic? The titles people use and the one their employers used might be different. When challenged, the applicant might say, "Well, they called me a clerk, but I really did a manager's job." That may be true, but check it out.

- Does the applicant demonstrate how acquired skills fit into the position sought? Can you see the transferability of skills? Are parameters provided so you can see the extent of responsibility? These parameters might include number of staff supervised, control over budget, or size of sales goals met.

As you review this material, compare résumé information with your ideal candidate. No one will meet all of the qualifications, but it will be a good place to begin.

RÉSUMÉ EVALUATION (Continued)

Other relevant activities

You may find a wide variety of information in this category. These might include college activities, community involvement, awards, church-related functions, hobbies, and participation in sports. All of these provide insight into the type of person the applicant is.

At first you may not think this information is relevant to the applicant's job abilities. Recognize that many of the skills learned in school or community activities can be transferred to your place of work. See sample résumé review on page 55.

Leadership positions in high school or college assist a person in developing the insight and understanding of work roles. Participation in sports helps gain confidence. Other outside activities develop maturity and character.

Figure 19—Sample résumé review

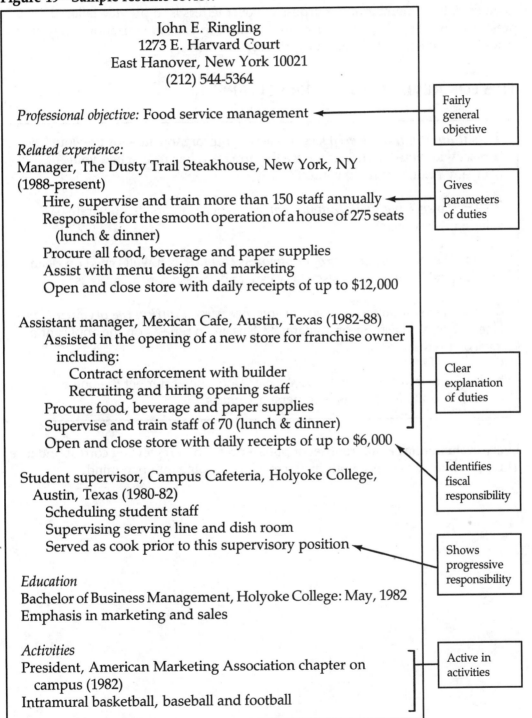

John E. Ringling
1273 E. Harvard Court
East Hanover, New York 10021
(212) 544-5364

Professional objective: Food service management ◄———— | Fairly general objective |

Related experience:
Manager, The Dusty Trail Steakhouse, New York, NY
(1988-present)
    Hire, supervise and train more than 150 staff annually ◄—— | Gives parameters of duties |
    Responsible for the smooth operation of a house of 275 seats
      (lunch & dinner)
    Procure all food, beverage and paper supplies
    Assist with menu design and marketing
    Open and close store with daily receipts of up to $12,000

Assistant manager, Mexican Cafe, Austin, Texas (1982-88)
    Assisted in the opening of a new store for franchise owner
      including:
        Contract enforcement with builder
        Recruiting and hiring opening staff
    Procure food, beverage and paper supplies
    Supervise and train staff of 70 (lunch & dinner)
    Open and close store with daily receipts of up to $6,000

(Clear explanation of duties)

(Identifies fiscal responsibility)

Student supervisor, Campus Cafeteria, Holyoke College,
  Austin, Texas (1980-82)
    Scheduling student staff
    Supervising serving line and dish room
    Served as cook prior to this supervisory position ◄—— | Shows progressive responsibility |

Education
Bachelor of Business Management, Holyoke College: May, 1982
Emphasis in marketing and sales

Activities
President, American Marketing Association chapter on
  campus (1982)
Intramural basketball, baseball and football

(Active in activities)

EVALUATING COVER LETTERS

Cover letters can provide additional insight into applicants' attitudes and abilities to do the job. Remember, the purpose of cover letters is to provide tailored presentations of applicants' background relative to your organization. They serve as an introduction to the interview process.

TIPS FOR REVIEWING COVER LETTERS.

1. *Is it an original letter?* Does it refer to your organization or previous contact with you? Is there evidence the applicant has researched your company prior to making contact?

2. *Are the spelling and grammar correct?* These factors demonstrate basic skills and show care.

3. *Has it been written in proper business format?* Is it well-typed on clean crisp paper? These factors also show care and respect for the process.

4. *Is the letter addressed to you or another person within the organization?* Does it begin, ''Dear Sir or Madame''? This again reflects on the applicant's level of interest.

5. *Does the letter achieve its objective?* Does the writer get the point across? Does it blend focus with persuasiveness?

Every evaluator has a different set of preferences when reviewing correspondence. The best strategy is to use your instincts while keeping an open mind.

Figure 20—Sample cover letter

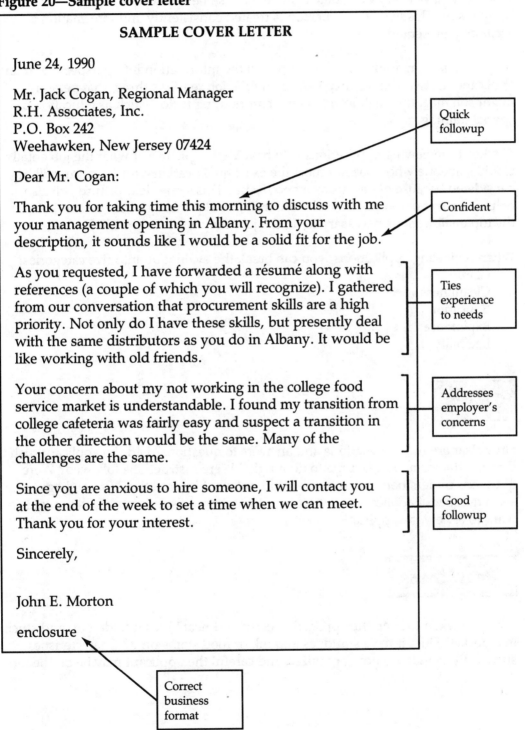

SAMPLE COVER LETTER

June 24, 1990

Mr. Jack Cogan, Regional Manager
R.H. Associates, Inc.
P.O. Box 242
Weehawken, New Jersey 07424

Dear Mr. Cogan:

Thank you for taking time this morning to discuss with me your management opening in Albany. From your description, it sounds like I would be a solid fit for the job.

As you requested, I have forwarded a résumé along with references (a couple of which you will recognize). I gathered from our conversation that procurement skills are a high priority. Not only do I have these skills, but presently deal with the same distributors as you do in Albany. It would be like working with old friends.

Your concern about my not working in the college food service market is understandable. I found my transition from college cafeteria was fairly easy and suspect a transition in the other direction would be the same. Many of the challenges are the same.

Since you are anxious to hire someone, I will contact you at the end of the week to set a time when we can meet. Thank you for your interest.

Sincerely,

John E. Morton

enclosure

Quick followup

Confident

Ties experience to needs

Addresses employer's concerns

Good followup

Correct business format

REVIEWING AN APPLICATION

When you have every candidate complete the same application, it eases comparison. This way, every person is treated consistently and information is accurately presented.

As you review an application, try to put all the information into perspective. If an applicant has two years of experience and the job requires three, that person might still meet the qualifications with contributing factors such as education or special training.

The key to reviewing applications is to have a clear picture of what the job entails. Could someone who does not meet the exact qualifications, for instance, still be considered because of enthusiasm and desire? This same clear picture will also help you ferret out applicants who are trying to slip through the system. Look at the top qualifications necessary to do the job; they are your priority.

When reviewing applications, you can break the evaluation into five categories:
        Clarity
        Cleanliness
        Education
        Experience
        Legibility

Clarity

How clear are the explanations and answers to questions? Did the applicant rush through the form, or take time to do it right? Were instructions followed? Were questions understood and answered with relevant information? (If you begin to see a number of applications where questions were misunderstood, you might want to review the application itself.)

Cleanliness

Was care taken to keep the application clean and neat? Was it folded up and stuck in a pocket? Does it have smudges and ink or food stains on it? Characteristics such as these indicate how organized and careful the applicant may be on the job.

Legibility

Can the handwriting be read? Does it fit in the lines? Are there a lot of crossouts or erasures? (This may indicate that the applicant is altering information.) Can you understand what is being expressed? All of these factors comment on the applicant's care and diligence.

Experience

Does the experience offered match the experience required for the job? How is it explained? Can you get a good idea of a person's duties from the description? Does it sound reasonable? Once again, remember that many skills are transferrable. Be careful not to dismiss a qualified candidate because of lack of an exact match.

Education

As with experience, you need to check for credibility. Does it seem consistent? Are the courses relevant to what you are looking for? Has this person completed certain levels of education? This would indicate follow-through.

Remember, only facts that are job-related may be evaluated! For instance, handwriting might be illegible, or there might be a number of spelling errors. These factors can be considered only if the job requires legible writing and communication skills, such as completing forms or writing reports.

DECIDING ON FINALISTS

Once you have gathered all the applications or résumés, create a simple form with the pertinent criteria listed across the top with the applicants' names down one side. This type of organization will help you make a clear comparison. You might develop a weighted scale (such as 1-5), and select according to a cutoff level. Be careful not to be too strict. You don't want to eliminate good candidates before you speak with them. Consistency and impartiality are the keys to this process.

INTERVIEWING EFFECTIVELY

ESTABLISHING THE PROCESS

Of all the selection methods available, interviewing is relied upon most heavily. It is also the most difficult to master.

The typical interview consists of questions about one's work history, education, desires and skills. But there is more to an interview than just what questions to ask. The non-verbal communication between the screener and the candidate, the depth of the answers, and a host of other factors all create a picture from which the candidate can be evaluated.

To make the most of interviewing candidates, you must first establish a process that can be followed consistently by all involved. Consider the following factors:

Who will be conducting the interviews? Those interviewing should have a direct role with the position. These roles should include the position's direct supervisor, the supervisor's boss, and perhaps managers who have substantial contact with the person in the position. Simply adding other company officials for political reasons is generally not wise and can be very time consuming.

When will the interviews take place? Select a schedule for hiring and stay with it. Clear interviewers' calendars in advance of scheduling candidates. Following a consistent timetable with all applicants sends the message that the position is important and not just something the company will get around to doing.

Where will the interviews take place? Consider the different options. You could conduct the first interview in a managers' office. The second interview might take place in a plant setting if you're a manufacturer, or in a store if you're a retailer. If the position involves a significant amount of phone work, a phone interview would be appropriate.

Be innovative about where you decide to conduct interviews. Watching candidates react to the environment they may be working in can reveal a lot about them.

What information would you like to obtain from each candidate? Define in advance the information you need to make clear decisions. Don't settle for whatever the candidate offers. You are making an important decision based on these interviews. Ask what you need to know. (More about questions later in the chapter.)

ESTABLISHING THE PROCESS
(Continued)

Figure 21—Interview priority checklist

INTERVIEW PRIORITY CHECKLIST

Position _____ Dept. _____

Using the job description as a reference, list the skills and characteristics you feel the successful candidate needs to possess. Be sure that every factor you list is job-related. When you have listed all skills and characteristics, weight each according to its level of importance to the success of the job. 1=low, 5=critical. When you have completed this form, use it to develop interview questions and screening tools for the selection process.

Priority	Skills and Characteristics	Weight

Total weight =

How many rounds of interviews will there be? Refrain from making a marathon out of the process. More than three interviews is probably counterproductive. Different interviewers should ask different questions. Asking the candidate to respond to the same questions over and over accomplishes little.

What purpose will each of these rounds serve? Determine in advance why you need each round of interviews. In many cases, two can suffice. Do not make the mistake of conducting the first round with 20 candidates. This elongates the process of narrowing the field. If you do have an extraordinary number of qualified people, conduct a round of phone screenings before asking anyone to the office.

How will screening decisions be made? Decisions should be made in a clear and organized fashion. Develop a simple evaluation form that can be used by everyone involved. While gut feeling plays a role in any decision, attempting to quantify your decision as much as possible makes for a clearer outcome and probably more accurate decision.

QUESTIONS TO ASK

The questions you ask and how you ask them largely determine the outcome of any interview. Therefore, these questions should be carefully designed to solicit as much information as possible.

Remember that all questions should be job related. Even simple discussions around the candidates' spouses and children might be construed as seeking discriminatory information. If you think you're asking something discriminatory, you probably are.

As you begin to develop questions, review the job description to determine the actual criteria for which you should be hiring. These criteria should provide you with the basis for most questions.

Be sure to include a question about the candidates' aspirations. While their ideas may not totally match what you have in mind, their answers will shed light on levels of ambition, focus and enthusiasm. How the candidates see your job fitting into their plans will have a great deal of influence on their desire for the position.

Ask candidates to tell you why they are interested in the position. Their responses will provide insight into their understanding of the position, the match with their skills, and how much they have researched your organization.

Questions regarding education should revolve around how a candidate's training applies to the position. Again, you must be careful about appearing discriminatory. It would not be a good idea, for example, to ask cashier applicants about their writing skills, since the ability to express oneself on paper is not a significant part of the job. On the other hand, you may ask about how they feel the courses they have taken address the skills needed for the job.

Questions about experience also must be job related. Base your questions on how they performed, not just what they did. Give them situations to solve and pose questions that make them think about how the problem could be solved in your environment. Whether they answer the question the same way you would is irrelevant; it's how they arrived at their solutions that counts. (Appendix A contains a selection of questions from which to choose.)

In addition to questions about goals, education and experience, you may choose to ask about work habits and attitudes. How well does the candidate get along with others? Will this person fit into your work environment? Is this person flexible and adaptable? You may be able to glean quite a bit regarding these characteristics from the way other questions are answered.

CONSIDER THE SETTING

In addition to developing questions, you should consider the setting in which the interview will take place. A lot of distractions and noise inhibits your ability to concentrate. While a plant or site tour might be an appropriate second interview, you want to concentrate on what the candidates say during the first meeting.

Try to prevent interruptions during the interview. They will destroy concentration, and candidates may interpret interruptions as a message that you don't care. If interruptions cannot be prevented in your office, find another location.

Arrange for plant or site tours in advance. There is nothing more embarrassing than arriving on site only to discover that the guide was not informed or there is nothing going on that can be observed. Once again, disorganization sends the wrong message.

In any interview, begin by putting the candidate at ease. As in any unfamiliar situation, the candidate will be somewhat uncomfortable. A little small talk, the offer of a beverage, or a light joke helps ease the tension.

CONDUCTING THE INTERVIEW

Begin by outlining the process. Explain the sequence of events that will happen in the interview. Refrain from defining the amount of time you will spend. If things are not going well after 15 minutes of a 45 minute interview, it may be difficult to end.

Keep an open mind. Your first impression of a candidate is usually lasting, but don't let it overshadow everything else in the interview. Some very good candidates may be nervous and give a less than positive impression until they relax.

Let the candidate do the talking. Refrain from talking so much about the job or company that the candidate does not get an opportunity to talk. The more people talk, the more insight you will gain into their personalities.

Be careful not to explain questions as you're asking them. You may give away the answer without knowing it. Stick to short, open-ended questions such as, ''How would you describe your leadership style?''

Remain attentive. When you are conducting a series of interviews, it is easy to get distracted by other concerns on the job or perhaps by fatigue. Do not let boredom overtake you.

Take notes while the candidate is talking. While you do not want to become preoccupied, what you write down will help you recall events later on.

If you feel like you're losing attentiveness, try paraphrasing what the candidate says. The candidate might say, ''My last boss left a lot of things up to me.'' In response to that, you might say, ''So you had a lot of responsibility.''

By paraphrasing, the candidate knows you are paying attention and you are becoming more involved in the conversation without dominating it. In addition, this technique usually encourages the candidate to expound on whatever you paraphrased, giving you even more information.

Observe body language. Besides listening to what is being said, watch how it is being said. Is there a level of enthusiasm? Does the person ask a lot of questions? Is there good eye contact? Does this individual sound invested in the job? Since nonverbal actions represent the majority of communication, attune yourself to these factors.

Maintain control. Be careful not to allow the candidate to take over the interview. Some enthusiastic individuals may attempt to get the better of you by asking lots of questions or making editorial comments rather than answering the questions.

In other situations, you may let time get away from you. Stick to the schedule unless there are extraordinary circumstances.

Probe incomplete answers. Sometimes the answer offered does not address the question. You may feel the candidate is hiding something. Ask more questions to ferret out the information. You may find this process uncomfortable, especially if you catch the candidate in a lie. This is better, however, than hiring the wrong person into the job.

Close on a positive note. End the interview on a positive note without announcing a decision. Keep your reaction to yourself and simply assure the candidate that you will be in touch within a short period of time.

Write an interview summary immediately after completing the interview. Record your general impressions along any questions or concerns you may have about the candidate. Waiting even one hour will greatly reduce your recall of the events. See the Interviewer's Self-Rating Sheet—page 68.

Consider alternative interview strategies. In addition to the traditional interview, a number of companies are using alternative strategies to gather information. Some companies are now asking top management candidates to complete projects that will demonstrate the ability for self-expression and organization.

Others ask individuals to make presentations, especially if the position requires this type of work. Still others provide typical situations the candidate might be faced with and ask the candidate to solve the problem.

Targeted selection systems are also gaining popularity. Instead of asking questions like, ''Tell me about yourself,'' the targeted question asks candidates to explain how they resolved a particular type of situation. Even if you do not agree with how the situation was handled, you gain insight into the candidates' problem-solving skills.

CONDUCTING THE INTERVIEW
(Continued)

Figure 22—Interviewer's Self Rating Form

INTERVIEWER'S SELF RATING

Interviewer _____ Date _____

Candidate interviewed_____ Position _____

Evaluation: 5 = Handled smoothly   4 = Handled well but needs refining
              3 = Has a grasp but needs   2 = Needs significant work
                   improvement   1 = Found this difficult

_____ Rapport with candidate

_____ Opened the interview and made the candidate feel at ease

_____ Avoided direct criticism of candidate

_____ Listened sympathetically

_____ Put the candidate at ease in awkward situations

Control of the interview

_____ Developed questions in advance of the interview

_____ Maintained the focus of the interview

_____ Made smooth transition from one topic to another

_____ Allocated time appropriately

_____ Returned to the original question when answer evasive

_____ Paced interview well

Persuaded candidate to elaborate on responses by using:

_____ Follow-up questions

_____ Silence

_____ Paraphrases of applicant's initial response

Note-taking

_____ Took notes discreetly during interview

_____ Did not allow note-taking to interfere with interview

_____ Noted dress and appearance if relevant

_____ Reviewed and summarized notes for follow-up

For clerical and staff positions, some companies are beginning to ask for a two-day trial period where the top candidates spend two days on the job interacting with other employees (and being paid for it, of course). Are candidates willing to take a couple of vacation days if currently employed? Their reactions might indicate what they would be like as employees.

Other companies give candidates situations to solve or short tasks to accomplish. These strategies provide insight into candidates' skills and dispositions.

Finally, organizations are returning to testing clerical skills, since these skills are becoming more complex. Too many organizations have been burned by individuals who said they could do something and really couldn't. Don't ask. Test!

SELLING THE ORGANIZATION'S IMAGE

Part of your job in an interview is to sell candidates on working for your organization. Remember that it is a two-way street: you're evaluating them and their evaluating you.

Communicate the organization's best point. You might even want to have a small "cheat sheet" to refer to when describing the company. Make sure any recruiting literature you have is polished and professional.

Be prepared to respond to their questions. Put yourself in their place for a second and understand how they might think. The candidates you want will ask the toughest questions because they care the most and have done the most research.

Figure 23—Selling the company

SELLING POINTS OF OUR COMPANY

As much as the candidates are trying to convince us to hire them, we need to persuade the top candidates to work for us. The points below will provide you with some information on the company that makes us more attractive to work for. While it is important to sell the company, make sure you are selling it to the right people. Try not to lead applicants on and be careful about making commitments you or the company cannot keep.

In explaining the company, have you mentioned that:

We are a growing company with plenty of upward potential. Our revenues have increased more than 50% per year for each of the last three years.

Our benefits program covers eye and dental care and there is no employee contribution, other than a three dollar co-pay per visit.

We have a stock ownership program for all employees.

We reimburse employees for all classes completed at approved colleges, provided they achieve a grade of "B" or better.

We are considered one of the largest suppliers of cleaning equipment and supplies on the East coast.

We offer flex time for a number of our positions.

EVALUATING THE CANDIDATES

Once the interviews are over, it is time to make some decisions. The best way to do this is to develop a simple evaluation sheet as you did for reviewing applications and résumés. Outline the criteria down the side and the candidates' names across the top. In some instances, one or two candidates will stand out above the rest and the decision will be obvious. In other cases, it will be a close call. In these situations a weighted system for evaluation will be helpful. (An example can be found on page 72). You cannot pass everyone on to the next round.

Be careful to avoid bias. Candidates should be evaluated on their merits as related to the job criteria. While there is room for some gut instinct, it should not overrule other important information.

Be timely in making the decision. Stay with the schedule you have announced to the candidates. Falling behind due to distractions or uncertainty can prove costly when your best candidate takes another job or accepts a position with your competitor.

SELLING THE ORGANIZATION'S IMAGE (Continued)

Figure 24—Interview Evaluation

INTERVIEW EVALUATION

Applicant_____ Telephone _____

Applying for _____

Interviewer _____ Date _____

List, in priority order, all the skills and characteristics necessary to perform the job. This information should be taken from the interview priority form. When you have completed this form, make a copy for each candidate to be interviewed.

Ratings: 1 = unacceptable for this position 5 = Exceeds requirements

Required skills/Characteristics	Rating

Total Rating =

Preferred skills/characteristics	Rating

Total Rating =

THE TESTING OPTION

Testing as a selection method is regaining popular acceptance. While still controversial in some cases, the business community is beginning to include pre-employment screening in its battery of hiring tools.

Pre-employment screening can be divided into two categories:

Psychological screening determines applicants skills, honesty and mental attitudes toward work. So-called paper and pencil tests are generally applied sometime during the beginning of the selection process and are used quite regularly to eliminate applicants prior to the first round of interviews. These tests take many forms and some have become relatively inexpensive to use.

Physical screening determines fitness to perform on the job. These tests include drug and alcohol, AIDS, and genetic screening. Where paper and pencil tests are conducted at the beginning of the process, physical screenings are generally conducted at the end as a condition of employment. In other words, ''We would like to offer you the job, but you must pass the physical screening first.'' The purpose of this timing is to avoid invasion of privacy complaints and to reduce costs.

Testing should serve a specific purpose in your hiring process. Testing for the sake of testing is both expensive and potentially dangerous legally. Before including any sort of screening in your selection process, you must develop a clear understanding of its role and desired outcomes.

The three major considerations in the use of testing are legality, cost and organizational commitment. Let's examine each:

Legality: All paper and pencil testing must pass the hurdles of validity, business necessity and potential adverse impact. Validity means that the test must measure what it is supposed to measure. Packaged tests for skills, honesty, and personality have been validated before being placed on the market. (More about this later.)

The employer must also be able to demonstrate that the skills or characteristics measured are a business necessity. For instance, you may not require a retail store applicant to pass a writing test unless you can demonstrate that there will be extensive writing required on the job.

THE TESTING OPTION (Continued)

Figure 25—Legalities of drug screening

LEGALITIES OF DRUG SCREENING

- There are no federal laws regulating drug screening.

- Currently, California, Connecticut, Iowa, Minnesota and Vermont are the only states with laws regulating drug screening although several are debating it. Consult with counsel before introducing such a program.

- Employers within the jurisdiction of federal, state or local antidiscrimination may risk disparate impact. (In other words, the screening has an unfair impact on one or more protected classes of applicants.)

- Unionized employers should recognize that the initiation of a drug screening program must be included in collective bargaining.

Physical screenings also face these three hurdles. The tests must measure what they are supposed to measure. The test must be shown to be a business necessity and must not have a disparate impact on protected groups.

Cost: While a three-dollar drug screening or honesty test may not appear to be costly at first, these expenses can add up when other considerations are added. On the physical side, inaccuracies running as high as 50 percent are common among the less expensive drug screenings. This requires a confirmation screening that is more accurate, but also more expensive. Over a one-year period, this can run into thousands of dollars.

Screening a large portion of applicants on the paper and pencil side is a common practice among some companies and can also run up the cost of testing. While you may screen three finalists for drugs and alcohol, the company may screen 20 or more applicants for honesty or basic skills. Add all of these costs together and testing can become a significant part of your recruiting budget.

Organizational reasoning: Finally, each organization must closely examine its motive for testing before beginning any program. What is the purpose of the screening program? What precipitated it? What are the expected outcomes? Is the organization committed to close monitoring and confidentiality? Are there legal ramifications that could cause time and expense? Is there an equally effective alternative?

PHILOSOPHY OF TESTING

It is totally up to the individual employer whether to screen physically or psychologically. While testing has been shown to be a reliable method for selection in some instances, it has also proven to be costly and time-consuming.

With much of its legality still to be decided by the courts, testing can be a legal land mine unless thoroughly researched and closely monitored upon implementation. Since it can be assumed that little, if any, information can be kept truly confidential in any organization, breech of confidentiality can also pose challenges.

Testing individuals can run from $3-$400 depending upon the type and accuracy of the method. This may be prohibitive for some companies. Many organizations that require drug and alcohol screenings ask the applicant to submit to a physical prior to employment, since placing the screening within the examination diffuses some of the controversy.

PAPER AND PENCIL TESTS

Paper and pencil tests can be broken into two categories:

- Honesty and personality testing
- Skills and aptitude testing

Honesty and personality tests are used to determine applicants' tendency toward honesty and how well they would get along in the job and work environment. Skills and aptitude testing measure one's ability to perform certain tasks such as typing, math calculation and writing.

Accuracy has been the main controversy surrounding paper and pencil tests. Some critics maintain that applicants who answer too honestly may be disqualified while individuals who know how to manipulate the tests will be accepted.

Applicants who do not "test" well are also sometimes disqualified when they would, in fact, make excellent employees. As mentioned above, tests that fail a higher than normal number of those in protected groups are considered discriminatory.

Finally, critics also maintain that pre-employment screening is an invasion of privacy and point to interviews, résumés and applications as reasonable means for gathering information.

Written honesty and personality tests are being used more widely since employers may no longer use the polygraph (lie detector) as a pre-employment screening device. The purpose of these tests is to measure an applicant's propensity for being honest. While they are not fool-proof, studies have found a strong correlation between those who are considered "high risk" by the tests and those who were found to steal on the job.

These tests usually consist of multiple choice, true/false and yes/no questions. The tests come with a booklet and answer sheet and range in price from $5 to $14. These instruments contain a "lie scale" to determine whether the applicant is trying to manipulate the test. A question of this nature might be, "I never think about stealing something from my employer." Since it might be assumed that some temptation to steal passes through everyone's mind at one point or another, a person who answers true might be attempting to manipulate the test.

Skills and aptitude testing measure the applicant's ability to perform a task or use a skill. Where honesty and personality testing generally consists of standardized instruments, skills and aptitude testing is a combination of published tests such as a typing battery and tests created by the employer to measure a specific skill.

You, as the employer, must be very careful to make sure that the tests you develop are valid and non-discriminatory. These tests do not have to be written in form. They might be physical measures such as coordination, lifting and assembly.

In order to be valid, the test must pass one of the three validation techniques approved by the Equal Employment Opportunity Commission's guidelines for validation. Check with your local district office for additional information.

Handwriting analysis is another screening device that is gaining acceptance in the United States. While this method of evaluation has been popular in Europe for years, it is relatively new to our country. It involves a review of the physical characteristics of one's handwriting compared with correlated samples of other individuals'. As with most testing, critics argue that this technique has no scientific basis. Analysis of this type runs from $25-$400.

If you choose to conduct pre-employment honesty, personality and skill testing, follow these recommendations:

- Check both federal and local regulations on pre-employment testing before proceeding.
- Check references of testing services and those supplying instruments.
- Make sure that each test you use is measuring what you want it to measure.
- Be sure that all testing you do is validated, especially those created by your organization.

DRUG AND ALCOHOL TESTING

Recent studies indicate that drug and alcohol screening is beginning to gain widespread acceptance among American employers. This is largely due to decreases in productivity, absenteeism and accidents on the job.

The controversy over drug testing revolves around invasion of privacy, poor levels of accuracy and safety in the work place. Regardless of your feelings about drugs, you as the employer have a legal responsibility to maintain a safe work place while still remaining within the law.

At this point there are no federal laws governing testing for drugs or alcohol in the work place. While some states have legislated applicants' rights to privacy, none has specifically prohibited drug testing. It is best in all situations to consult with your attorney before commencing with pre-employment screening for drugs and alcohol.

The **procedures for testing** are rather complex. A basic understanding of the concepts would be helpful here.

Most employers screening for substance abuse use urine testing as their initial procedure. More sophisticated methods involve blood, breath, skin, hair and saliva.

The most common test used by laboratories providing these services is ''enzyme multiplied immunoassay,'' which measures the reaction of the urine specimen to radioactive animal antibodies. This reaction indicates a presence of drugs.

The most accurate of these tests is the ''gas chromatography mass spectrometry'' (GC-MS) test. This is used to confirm the presence of drugs, since many initial screenings have such a high error rate.

A confirmation test should always be performed in the case of a positive reaction, due to the chance of a false positive sometimes created by the use of certain over the counter drugs.

Drug screenings will identify other medications the applicant may be using for such conditions as depression or epilepsy. Be careful not to evaluate applicants based on this information, since it may be an invasion of privacy or protected under handicapped legislation.

A crucial part of any drug screening program is the selection of a laboratory. Be careful to check references and ask to see the facilities in which the work will be done. It is also important to execute an agreement emphasizing confidentiality. This contract should contain a "hold harmless" clause making the laboratory, and not your organization, liable for negligence in the event of litigation.

Any applicant who tests positively should be given the opportunity for a confirming test to assure accuracy, even if this is at the applicant's expense.

When deciding to conduct pre-employment drug and alcohol screening, follow these guidelines:

- Conduct the screenings as part of an overall physical.
- Check laboratory references thoroughly before proceeding.
- Test only those who have reached the final stages of selection.
- Have all applicants sign a release if at all possible. Make sure that they understand their refusal means automatic elimination from consideration.
- Applicants who fail the drug screening should be eliminated on the basis of not passing the physical.
- Absolute confidentiality must be maintained at all times.

DECIDING TO TEST

Simply considering the idea of pre-employment testing may create controversy within your organization. While honesty or skills screening might be fully accepted, testing for drugs is sure to stir issues.

The best way to deal with the potential controversies is to clearly determine in advance your reasons for testing, and the goals you wish to reach by using it. Is it to reduce theft, increase productivity, reduce absenteeism, or create a safer work environment?

Whatever your reasons, develop a clearly defined and consistent plan. Nothing alienates applicants and employees more than inconsistency in policy. It also opens you up to possible litigation and fines.

Follow the suggestions in this chapter and conduct thorough research on all aspects before proceeding.

CONDUCTING REFERENCE CHECKS

How often do you check the references of seriously considered applicants? It takes time and effort. Then you usually get only glowing recommendations and praise. You must conclude that all this investigating is a waste of time; still, you can glean valuable candidate information.

In addition to getting biased information, another issue to consider is the reluctance by some companies to provide information beyond employment dates and job titles. In this litigious society, an applicant who feels he's been slandered can sue a former employer for simply expressing an opinion about his performance.

Still, reference checking must play a crucial role in the selection process. It is not enough to rely on the word of the applicant, but getting the right information can be a challenge.

RESISTANCE FROM REFERENCES

Until recently, obtaining reference information was fairly easy. You called the former supervisor, asked a few questions, and received candid answers. While you may not have always received the information you were seeking, the average boss had little hesitation in giving an opinion.

Over the past decade, however, a number of employers have been sued successfully when former employees claimed the reference-givers made false statements about their performances. In some cases, the question or response may have been misconstrued. The result is that employers are watching their colleagues pay thousands of dollars in settlements and judgments.

Since many employers have begun to examine their practice of giving references, a number have developed policies prohibiting the release of information other than the employee's dates of employment and job title. In a growing number of cases, calling a supervisor for a reference will result in referral to human resources.

This obstacle to reference-checking is not as sweeping as some would have you believe. But apprehension about giving references does prevent the system from working.

To overcome this resistance, several strategies may be attempted:

- If you call the employee's department and are referred to human resources, try the department again later. If you get a different person the second time, you may get more information.

- If you are having little success, ask another member of your department to give it a try. Sometimes the rapport developed between the reference checker and reference giver makes all the difference.

- You might also call back and simply ask to speak with a person who has worked with the applicant. With an open question like this, you may get a willing response.

- Finally, if nothing else works, appeal to the reference's common sense. If all companies stop giving references for fear of being sued, the recruiting system will experience a grave loss.

QUESTIONS TO ASK

Preparation is the key to making the most out of a reference check. This inquiry must be conducted in a deliberate fashion. Questions should be developed around what you need to know by examining the job description and reflecting back on individuals who have held the position.

All questions should be job related. Drifting off into inquiries about lifestyles and personal information is asking for trouble.

There must be consistency between candidates. Asking different people different questions destroys your ability to compare. While all queries should be consistent, you should pursue inconsistencies in what the reference says, and seek clarification if a response arouses your curiosity.

Here are a typical set of questions you might ask:

- How long did Jack work for the company?
- What position did he hold when he left?
- What position did he begin in?
- How would you describe his work ethic?
- Given the opportunity, would you hire him again?
- What reservations should I have about hiring him?
- This is what he would be doing for our firm. How do you think his skills and abilities would fit into that position?
- Who else within your organization would be able to comment on his performance?
- What were his reasons for leaving your organization?

HOW TO ASK QUESTIONS

Because of our time pressures, there is always a temptation to rush through reference checks. Yet building rapport is one of the most important parts of conducting this type of inquiry. The impressions you get will be just as important as the facts. You need to develop a positive relationship with each reference.

Some references may be more hesitant about providing information than others. They may not, for instance, feel positively about the person in question. If you get an indication that they feel reluctant about certain topics, these may be areas you should pursue with other references and the applicant.

It is your job to make the references feel at ease. The more rapport you build, the more information you can obtain. Discipline yourself to hear not only what is being said, but how it is being said.

One means for getting additional information out of a reluctant reference is to rephrase the question:

Q: "How would you describe Janet's work ethic?"

A: "She did her job. . .got along with people."

Q: "So you would say that she approached her job with energy and enthusiasm."

A: "Uh. . .I guess you could say that."

As you can see in the exchange above, the first query did not get the desired results. So the questioner drew a conclusion to see how the reference would respond. While the reference verbally agreed with the conclusion, it was obvious that it lacked sincerity.

In this case the questioner might want to pursue the response by saying something like, "You don't sound too enthusiastic about Janet," but might incur the wrath of the reference by challenging the original response. If the questioner wants to obtain additional information on other topics, it is best to maintain the rapport and leave the question alone.

In some cases, you may have to manipulate a reference's impression in order to obtain the information you need. You might say, ''We're down to our finalists, and are trying to get the best match.'' From this statement, references may conclude that they have nothing to lose and therefore will be more candid in their responses.

Another question might be, ''Since this person will be going through some training once she's on board, I'm wondering where you think she would benefit the most?'' If the reference draws the conclusion that Janet already has the job, that person might be more forthcoming with relevant impressions.

It is up to you, as a reference checker, to provide many opportunities for the reference to open up. Remember, it is not just what is said, but how it is said.

EVALUATING REFERENCES

Once you have spoken with the references of all finalists, it is time to compare the results. Again, the key here is to remain impartial and consistent. If copious notes are taken during each reference check, you should have an accurate picture of how each candidate interacts with an employer, the reservations the employers have, and the points in favor of each candidate. Remember to include the non-verbal clues of the references in the evaluation. These sometimes form the key information on which to come to a conclusion.

Since reference checking is performed in the final stages of selection, the information you receive should serve to confirm conclusions already drawn on finalists. If however, you receive information about a candidate that needs checking, pursue it. Requesting an additional contact with a finalist may be uncomfortable, especially if this person appears the best choice, but you need to address all questions before making a decision.

CREDENTIAL AND CREDIT CHECKS

In addition to checking references, you may wish to verify other credentials. These might include education, training and credit.

It is not uncommon for some applicants to slightly or grossly exaggerate their educational credentials. Do not fool yourself into thinking that because some people have all the right answers that they also have the credentials. While most do, all should be checked. Some schools will release transcript data only at the written request of alumni. If this is the case, impress upon the applicant that you need the material promptly to expedite the hiring process.

When calling educational institutions, go a couple of steps beyond asking whether the applicants attended. Ask if they graduated and when. Check to see that the majors the candidates indicated on their applications are the same ones the schools credited them with.

Credit checks are appropriate only when the position being filled will involve money-handling or major fiscal responsibility. In other words, you may check the credit of a controller or cashier, but not of a production manager or sales person.

Information of this type is regulated by the Federal Fair Credit Reporting Act as well as many state laws. Consult with your attorney regarding what may be done in your locale.

With this information, you can gain some insight as to whether the candidate is experiencing financial difficulties. From these facts you may determine whether this person might be tempted to handle funds illegally or indiscreetly.

With this practice, you are protecting yourself not only against in-house loss and theft, but also against actions brought by others while the employee is acting in your behalf.

DECISION MAKING AND OFFERS

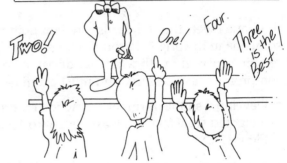

How clear is your decision making process for hiring? Whether you are selecting a chief executive officer or a cashier, the decision must be made carefully.

While many people go with their ''gut feelings,'' there is more to the process. Holding the fate of someone's job in your hands is not an easy task. You must make sure that both the organization and the employee are well served. But why do we have such a hard time deciding who to hire?

As with the rest of the hiring process, it helps to revisit the original criteria for the best candidate. Chances are, you have not found a perfect match. Your option at this time can be to reopen the search for candidates who better match the position's needs. If you have done a good job recruiting, however, the next group will not be any closer.

The better strategy, in most cases, is to compare the job description to your best two or three candidates. Flexibility is the key to making the hiring decision successful. Not only is searching for the perfect match usually unrealistic, it does not serve your organization well.

Employers who make a practice of hiring someone who can complete 80 percent of the job find that these new employees stay longer and feel more stimulated in the position. With proper training and support, these new employees can excel in the position.

DECISION MAKING PROCEDURES

Procedures for making the decision can vary widely according to your needs and the type of hire. Here are a few parameters to guide your selection:

- In making decisions, you have two options: comparing the candidates with each other or comparing each candidate against the stated criteria. Some maintain that comparing the candidates to each other is the better way to go since likening them to a standard may be unrealistic. Others maintain that comparing candidates may lower the standards you desire.

If no one meets the standards, are you going to re-open the search, or settle for someone in the original group? There is no right solution to this dilemma. But remain consistent with whatever decision you make. Keep in mind that when compromise is necessary, you must examine your priorities.

- Develop a simple form including job criteria, list of candidates and perhaps a weighted scale (such as 5 = excellent to 1 = poor), to allow comparison. (See Figure 26.)

- Maintain consistency when making decisions. Once all the information has been gathered, only those making the decision should be involved. Discourage outside lobbying.

- Recognize that strict job criteria should not be the only consideration. Every decision maker must allow for a little ''gut feeling.'' The new employee must be able to thrive in the environment and get along with others on the team. These factors are sometimes not clearly defined or demonstrated in job descriptions and interviews.

- Be able to explain your decision. Chances are you will be asked to justify your pick by a supervisor or co-workers. Your ability to clearly delineate your reasons will put to rest any uncertainty about the decision.

- For clerical and labor positions, one decision-maker is optimal. This person should be the position's immediate supervisor. For managerial jobs, a maximum of three persons should be involved. This should include the immediate supervisor and two other individuals with whom the person will work.

Figure 26—Candidate selection form

CANDIDATE SELECTION

Position _____ Start Date _____

Supervisor _____

Applicant's Name _____ Phone _____

Qualifications required	Comments	Rating

Qualifications desired	Comments	Rating

Evaluator _____ Date _____

SECURING THE BEST

As competition grows for skilled employees, you must develop effective strategies for landing your best candidates. While you might be used to taking your time deciding on offers, that luxury will no longer be available. Here are a few hints to enhance your hiring success:

- Share as much information as you can with your top applicants. It will give those people the opportunity to get to know your organization in depth.

- Establish a common interest. Ask about their desires, goals and aspirations. Discover their values and what they consider important. The more you are able to match their needs with yours, the better the match will appear.

- Organize your negotiating stand ahead of time. Consider all aspects of the package: vacation, salary, benefits, perks, budget control, influence on their destiny in the company and so on. Be prepared at all times to discuss the compensation and role that person will play in the organization.

- Use your intuition. If something does not feel right with a candidate, investigate. Better to uncover unpleasant facts now, rather than later.

- Use your sales pitch! Be prepared to persuade your top candidate. Don't go overboard and overwhelm. But try to convince this person that this is a good match, if you believe it.

- Don't make promises you can't deliver. No candidate is worth enough to exceed the bounds of common sense. If you're being asked for something you truly can't deliver, say so. Look for alternatives to satisfy the candidate's desires.

- Act quickly! The best candidates wait for no one. Keep the selection process moving, and keep your top candidates informed. The more they are involved in the process, the more they will be invested.

NOTIFICATION

Notifying candidates is one of the most crucial parts of the selection process. Just as you are examining them, they are examining you! Timely execution of the decision reassures your top applicants of your interest and renews their interest in the position.

One of the best ways to keep the process efficient is to announce a schedule to all candidates. This discourages the procrastination sometimes associated with selection. The entire process for any candidate should take no longer than three weeks.

Try to sell those involved on how productivity will increase and their time commitments will decrease once the new person is on. This should serve as an effective motivator. Keep them abreast of the process. If there is a delay in the process, a quick phone call to the finalists lets them know they're still being considered.

All applicants should be notified in a consistent manner. If one candidate is informed by phone that they were not selected, all candidates should be called. Everyone should be treated the same to avoid the appearance of bias or unfair treatment, and treating finalists consistently and openly leaves a good impression. You never know when your paths may cross again.

Every applicant who has been interviewed should receive a response. If eliminated, candidates should be notified within a week. Notification should take the form of a letter. Using post cards, as some employers do, is embarrassing and insensitive.

Figure 27—Rejection letter

REJECTION LETTER

Dear _____

Thank you for your interest in the position of _____ with our organization.

We received a great number of applications from qualified individuals and at this point, we have made a decision.

We will keep your application on file for six months in the event other applicable openings arise. Thank you for your understanding. We wish you the best in your job search.

Sincerely,

_____

MAKING THE OFFER

Timing is a very important part of making an offer. Once the decision has been made on a top candidate, contact that person immediately. More than one opportunity has been missed by delaying a day or two due to company bureaucracy.

Once you have made the offer, confirm it in a letter. Be careful not to include language in the letter that implies permanence or a guarantee of lifetime employment. All employees should be referred to as current or full-time, not permanent. In the letter, state the starting date, compensation, where to report and other specifics. Once again, welcome the candidate into the organization.

With highly skilled candidates and upper management you will probably negotiate at least a portion of the agreement. Here are a few tips:

• Know your parameters before discussing the offer with the candidate. Develop a list of possible offering points and stick to your plan. Don't "wing" the negotiations. It will cost you money and maybe the candidate.

Figure 28—Letter of Offer

LETTER OF OFFER

Dear _____

We enjoyed the opportunity to meet with you this past Wednesday. We are pleased to offer you the position of _____ .

This offer is contingent upon the following:

• A satisfactory physical exam

• Satisfactory references from your present employer

• Proof of authorization to work in the United States (Please bring these documents with you on the first day of work.)

Accepting this offer means that you will be performing the following duties and be responsible for _____ . Your salary would be $_____ monthly.

I hope you will accept this offer. We feel our organization provides excellent opportunities and working conditions along with a comprehensive benefits package.

I would like to have your decision by _____ . If you have any questions, feel free to call me at _____ . I look forward to your reply.

Sincerely,

_____

- Use incentives as bargaining points. There are a host of options from which to choose. In addition, you may tie compensation to performance, enabling the candidate to earn significantly more.

- Consider non-monetary perks. These might include a larger office, more control over vacation and other days off, latitude in project selection, and influence in decision-making.

- Get the candidate to commit before making the offer. Your posting may have asked for salary history or requirements, in which case you have a rough idea of expectations. A second strategy is to ask the candidate, ''What do you think you're worth?'' The response to this question will provide insight into how well the person has researched his or her own worth and how realistic the expectations are.

REFUSALS

Regardless of how hard you try, on occasion your top candidate will refuse the offer. If you have not received a response within two days of the offer, phone the candidate again to answer any questions and confirm an understanding of the offer.

If the candidate holds out for more compensation, you will have to negotiate. Be prepared before making this follow-up call. If more than one candidate is declining, you might want to reconsider your package and compensation. Ask candidates why they declined, and you may receive some useful information.

EMPLOYEE ORIENTATION AND TRAINING

ROLE AND VALUE OF ORIENTATION

Think back to the last time you took a new job. What kind of an orientation did you get? If you are like most people, it probably appeared somewhat disorganized and scattered.

In one office, you completed personnel forms. In another, you received a brief overview of job responsibilities, hours, pay schedule and vacation allowance. Then you were left to fend for yourself.

With the high cost of turnover, we can no longer afford to treat new employees this way. An employee's first impression of your firm should be one of quality, caring, organization and focus.

A person who begins with a clear picture of the job and defined expectations tends to excel. It is your job, as the employer, to ensure that this happens.

Begin by considering the first day of work from the new hire's point of view. How would you feel? What might you be expecting?

While you are enthusiastic about the job, you might also have some concerns about basic needs such as where to have lunch, the location of rest rooms, and where to get office supplies or tools.

Before conducting an orientation, you might ask the impressions of employees who have recently joined your organization. If they were to create an orientation, what would they include? Ask a couple to attend the session for new hires and speak about their experiences. New employees, seeing others who have made it, will feel better about joining the organization.

ROLE AND VALUE OF ORIENTATION
(Continued)

Regardless of the position for which a person is hired, there is a period of adjustment that has to take place. How well you, as the employer, assist in that transition determines how well that person will succeed in the job.

The first step is to make a list of those components essential to your orientation process. These might include information on the company and its mission, location of essential services, basic forms and policies, and general employee expectations. See page 99 for Figure 29—Sample Orientation Checklist.

Pass your list around to others in the organization and ask for input. This will get them invested in the orientation process. Once you have gathered all the information you need to conduct the process, design a program that provides new hires with necessary information and helps them feel a part of their new organization.

Begin the new employee's day about an hour later than the rest of the staff. This gives everyone involved with the orientation a chance to get organized. Let the receptionist know that a new person will be coming. The worst feeling in the world is to arrive on the first day and have the staff not know what to do with you.

You might start the orientation with an overview of the company and its mission. Simply distributing pamphlets will not do. Give a feel for why the organization is in business. Explain the role you serve and the role this new person will serve.

A welcoming visit by a senior manager would be more appropriate. Be sure however, that this person is well prepared and enthusiastic. You don't want to start off on the wrong foot.

Figure 29—Orientation checklist

Dear _____

We're glad you've joined our organization. As your supervisor takes you through the orientation process they will be covering a number of topics. This checklist is provided to ensure you are familiar with all the necessary information. Feel free to ask plenty of questions. We want your entry into our company to be as simple as possible!

____ Working hours	____ Attendance policy
____ Rate of pay	____ Dress code
____ Pay period, first pay	____ Telephone calls
____ Payroll deductions	____ Organizational structure
____ Benefits program	____ Tour of facility
____ Medical plan (dates eligible)	____ Parking
____ Emergency leave policy	____ Lunch areas
____ Work rules	____ "Buddy" assigned
____ Job description reviewed	____ Job evaluation
____ Discipline procedures	____ Termination policy
____ Introductory period	

Completed forms: ____ W-4   ____ Personal data form   ____ I-9
____ Waiver/designation of beneficiary for insurance plans

Special notes _____

_____

I understand the above are general guidelines and may be changed at any time as business requires. The information above does not constitute a written contract and I understand my employment is for no definite period of time and may be ended at will.

I acknowledge that we have discussed all of the above.

_____   _____
Employee signature/date   Supervisor signature/date

ROLE AND VALUE OF ORIENTATION (Continued)

You might then provide a tour of the site or plant. Introduce the new employee to as many people as possible and answer as many questions as possible. While new hires will not feel totally comfortable right away, they can at least discover the basic layout of the organization and develop some familiarity with who works where. See page 101 for Figure 30—Sample orientation memo.

After the tour is a good time to sit down and review general employee expectations and procedures. The manager who will be supervising this person should handle these details. The sooner the manager and employee get to know each other, the faster the transition will take place.

Benefit forms and other paperwork will have to be completed, but paperwork should not dominate the orientation.

Recognize that any orientation is somewhat stressful and confusing. If the orientation runs longer than expected, continue until finished.

You might arrange for a "buddy" system to assist this new employee in adjusting to the work environment. Choose a buddy with whom the new person can identify.

When conducting the orientation, take into consideration how the new employee may feel. You do not want to make this into a marathon of facts and introductions. Reinforce important points and leave plenty of time for questions. Orientation should be a time to acclimate to one's environment.

Periodically evaluate orientations. You might wait a month and then ask new employees about their impressions of how it was conducted. What went well? What was helpful? What was not helpful? How could it be improved? This feedback can be incorporated into the development of new orientations. The needs and concerns these employees express can also be considered in the actual hiring process.

Figure 30—Orientation memo

MEMORANDUM

TO: All managers
FROM: John Stanford, Director of Operations
RE: Tips on enhancing orientation

Here are a few ideas on how we can make the most of orienting new employees:

- Meet the employee at the front desk

- Provide a brief history of the organization including mission, organizational chart, products, position in the industry or field and anything you deem important.

- Give an organizational tour. Go into some depth, but not too much. Encourage questions and get to know the person on a personal level.

- Explain your department's function within the organization. What role does it play? How is it related to others? What departments are dependent on it? On what departments does it depend?

- Review the job description. Cover duties, authority, relationships with others in the department. Make sure this information is understood.

- Discuss attendance, tardiness, sickness, vacation and hours of work.

- Complete I-9, benefit and payroll forms.

- Introduce buddy. (Match this person with someone in your department to assist him/her in adjusting to new surroundings. Give it some thought and select a buddy ahead of time.

- Introduce this person to the staff member conducting training. If you will be conducting the training, set the schedule.

- In general, get all new hires involved in the department as soon as possible and make them feel at home and needed.

PRACTICAL CONSIDERATIONS

While orientation should be a time for introductions and enthusiasm about the new job, there are also a number of practical considerations.

Develop a checklist of the essential items that must be covered during the orientation of all new employees. These items include benefit forms, the I-9, and employee data forms. The example below provides a starting point.

Figure 31—Recordkeeping Form

PERSONAL DATA FORM

Name _____ Social Security # _____

Address _____

_____

Birthdate _____ Home Phone _____

Start date _____ Employee ID #_____

Initial and date the following when completed:

____ Application completed   ____ Life insurance forms

____ References checked   ____ ID card issued

____ W-4 (IRS) completed   ____ Employee handbook

____ I-9 (Immigration)   ____ Locker assigned

____ Orientation (by _____)   ____ Keys issued

____ Physical

____ Health insurance forms

Comments: _____

_____

_____

SETTING CLEAR EXPECTATIONS OF PERFORMANCE

One of the most important elements of orientation is the establishment of clear expectations. Take a considerable amount of time to review the job descriptions for new employees. Give them the opportunity to ask questions and consider each point. If you're unsure whether they understand, ask them some questions. It is better to discover misunderstandings now rather than later.

Also review other expectations of the job. These include work schedule, holiday and vacation schedule, and pay periods. The more employees know about their new surroundings and expectations, the more comfortable they will feel.

You might want to confirm these expectations with each employee in writing after the initial orientation. This may be contained in the organizational policy manual or in a memorandum to each new hire.

EMPLOYEE INTRODUCTORY PERIODS

Most organizations have established an introductory period for new hires. This period gives you the opportunity to observe the person in action and, at the same time, refrain from making a formal employment commitment.

Traditionally, these periods have been referred to as probation, but the courts have ruled that successfully completing a probation implies that the employee has become permanent. Since there should be no such thing as a permanent employee, the term probation should be avoided.

The expectations of introductory periods should be clearly explained to all new hires. Make sure you explain that even when the introductory period is over, the employees will not be permanent. They will be referred to as ''full-time'' or ''regular''.

As part of the orientation, new hires should meet with their supervisors to discuss specific duties and responsibilities. All employees should clearly understand what is expected of them from the very beginning. Explain how performance will be measured and allow them to ask questions. With some jobs, such as sales or assembly work, results are clearly measurable. Others, such as customer service representative or manager, are more of a challenge. With these positions, you might ask the new hire's opinion as to what is fair measurement and expectation. Once agreement has been reached, record it on a piece of paper and give the employee a copy.

The length of an introductory period depends upon the type of position. For an hourly worker, 30-60 days should be enough. With a managerial employee, up to a year might be appropriate depending upon the position's expectations and scope of control.

During this time, regular evaluations should be conducted with each new hire to determine progress and performance. If the supervisor or employee has any questions or concerns, this is when they should be discussed.

Problems should be addressed directly. Beating around the bush only confuses the new hire and makes for misunderstandings later on. Every session should be closed, with the supervisor summarizing what is going well, along with suggested areas for improvement. These discussions should be recorded in the employees's file in case there is a dispute at a later date.

While this process may sound complex and time consuming, it results in a clearer and more positive relationship with new employees.

TRAINING NEW EMPLOYEES

Providing new employees with the proper training helps to ensure their success on the job. The type and amount of training they receive depends upon several factors. These include:

Complexity of the duties. If you are training a cashier, there will not be as much initial instruction involved as with a technical service representative.

New hire's experience. If the new hire has experience, that person will adjust to the job faster than a novice.

Organizational retention rate. High turnover may be a significant factor in your business. An industry that retains its employees for a longer period of time may invest more in each employee. You may find that short, intense instruction, especially for some jobs, will reduce your training costs for new hires. A good example of this is the fast-food restaurant business, where turnover sometimes reaches 300 percent in one year.

Amount of money to invest in training. Some organizations are able to invest more money in training than others. If you are unable to do so, then low budget creativity becomes a significant consideration.

Developing actual training objectives involves assessing the type and amount of training needed, developing or purchasing the appropriate programs, and implementing these programs.

To assess the training needed for a particular job, begin by consulting the job description. Determine the skills that are necessary for working the job. Next consult with those employees actually performing the job. What would they recommend as training? How did they receive their training? What improvements would they make in the training they received?

The next step is to develop a training outline for the position and have it reviewed by those performing the job. This procedure gives you the objectives that need to be met for designing the training program.

Training programs can be developed for your individual needs, you may bring in outside trainers, or you may opt to use the packaged programs already on the market. These packages are available from a number of sources. The best way to discover your options is to peruse professional magazines such as *Training and Development Journal, Training Magazine, Human Resource Executive* and *HR Magazine.* Other professional journals in your field will also contain suggestions.

TRAINING NEW EMPLOYEES
(Continued)

When examining these programs, consider the following questions:

- Does the program address the topics you need to cover?

- Is the material up-to-date?

- Are these topics covered in a manner that your employees would be receptive to?

- Do similar firms use this program and do they find it effective?

- Does it fall within your budget?

- Is there solid customer support?

- Will you be required to purchase additional support materials such as workbooks and assessment tools?

If you do choose to develop your own programs, there are several considerations:

Cost: In this calculation, include professionals' development and presentation time, printing of materials, and outside support materials. Divide the number of participants taking this program into the calculation. That will give you a rough cost per participant.

Delivery: Consider who will deliver this program. Will it be the individual supervisors? An outside consultant? The training department? Will this be a quality delivery? If so, you will probably have to train each instructor.

Time consumption: How much time will this program consume from your schedule and others? It's not just the cost that is an obstacle. You have many other priorities. Which come first?

Maintaining currency: Will the program require constant up-dating? Technical programs sometimes do. How much trouble will it be to periodically re-work this program as opposed to purchasing a package program or having an outside consultant perform the service?

If you choose to develop and deliver your own programs, there are a host of organizational resources at your disposal. They include:

- American Society for Training and Development
- Employment Management Association
- National Society for Performance & Instruction
- National Speakers' Association
- Society for Human Resource Management
- Your industry's professional associations

If you choose to contract with outside trainers, here are a few brief guidelines:

- Have a clear picture in your mind of what you would like consultants to do before contacting them.
- Research typical fee schedules and arrangements in advance. Remember, hiring an inexpensive consultant who does not accomplish the task is worse than paying more for one who does.
- Ask for referrals from trusted colleagues.
- Check with several consultants before hiring. Don't hire the first one you like.
- Check to see if the consultant has performed the type of training you are seeking.
- Ask for samples of the consultant's work from other engagements.
- Have a written contract.

RETENTION

Even with proper orientation and training, your organization will still experience a degree of turnover. While the loss of employees cannot be completely eliminated, there are some simple steps you can use to increase retention:

Ask for employee input. Employees like to be included and more than one company has found that those on the front line have the best ideas for solving problems and developing better strategies. Take advantage of this valuable resource.

Stay in touch with employees' needs. Employee needs change constantly due to turnover, technology and a host of individual reasons. Paying attention to these needs is one of the most effective means for maintaining loyalty and productivity, not to mention a solid corporate image in the community.

Keep everyone informed. One of the top concerns in any employee survey is the need to know what's going on. Employees want to hear the bad news as well as the good. Sharing all issues with staff helps foster a sense of trust.

Conduct exit interviews. While you will not hold on to everyone, conducting exit interviews is one of the best means for discovering problems and concerns within the work force. Exiting employees have nothing to lose and will therefore sometimes share information you would not have been able to obtain otherwise.

CLOSING THOUGHTS

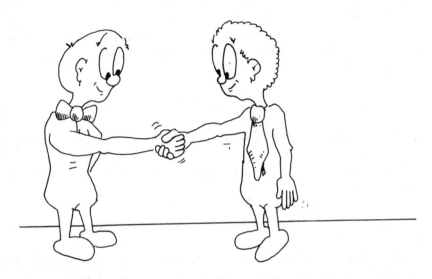

High performance hiring will be the only alternative for companies to excel in the future. Traditional trial and error of staff selection is no longer effective. Rather than viewing employee selection as a monumental task, integrate its functions into your everyday duties.

Always be on the lookout for talent and enthusiasm. Have clear knowledge of all positions under your authority. Be prepared to hire individuals quickly and decisively. Selection does not have to be the elongated process it is made out to be. Attack employee selection with energy and focus.

Attracting attention to your company also attracts applicants. Continually polish corporate image. Be prepared to talk about the organization and possible openings. If someone shows interest, conduct an informal interview. If you like what you see, ask for some contact information. You may not be aware of an opening right now...but it might be waiting for you when you return to the office. So keep your candidate files up to date. Work to create the corporate image necessary to attract applicants. By being the company to work for you, you will have your choice of the top performers.

High performance hiring requires investment. But like all good investment, it pays off in the long run with a rich selection of applicants.

Following is a checklist for developing a game plan for high performance hiring. Some of these pieces may already be in place where you work, but success requires completion of the formula!

HIGH PERFORMANCE HIRING CHECKLIST

☐ Can you clearly explain your organization's philosophy of hiring? (i.e., "Since our industry is prone to high turnover, we concentrate 40 percent of our recruiting budget on promotions and community activities to keep our name in front of possible applicants. We reward long term workers to keep them motivated."

☐ Do you have up-to-date job descriptions for all positions you supervise?

☐ Are you able to explain current openings to prospective candidates?

☐ Do you have an understanding of federal legal requirements and the intent of the law?

☐ Are you knowledgeable about local and state legal requirements?

☐ Can you clearly describe the "right recruit" for your organization? This includes work ethic, values, interests, and basic skills.

☐ Have you established an effective system for recruiting internally? Ten percent of openings per year should be filled by internal candidates.

☐ Do you have a budget set aside for external recruiting that meets your goals for attracting applicants?

☐ Have you identified your applicant needs for the next 24 months?

☐ Are you conscientiously pursuing these applicant pools?

☐ Have you identified the mediums that work best for attracting applicants to different openings?

☐ Have you examined alternative advertising mediums in addition to the traditional methods?

☐ Have you conducted a survey of applicants to determine their perception of your organization's image?

☐ Have you identified applicant's motivations for the positions you hire for?

☐ Have you developed a system for reviewing résumés that uncovers the information you need?

☐ Have you developed a system for reviewing applications that uncovers the information you need?

☐ Do you have a system for deciding on finalists after the applications and résumés have been reviewed?

☐ Have you developed a system for checking references?

☐ Have you developed a system for checking credentials and credit if applicable?

☐ Have you defined the information you need from an interview and established a process that uncovers this information on a consistent basis?

☐ Are the others involved in the selection process clearly trained on interview techniques and application review?

☐ Have you developed a system for selling organizational image when in contact with clients?

☐ Have you established a process for making interview decisions?

☐ Have you examined the option of whether to test applicants and make a determination?

☐ If yes, have you developed a reliable system for achieving the data you need?

☐ Have you developed a system for making final decisions, making offers and negotiating compensation?

☐ Have you established a thorough orientation program for each position?

☐ Have you established a thorough training program for each position?

☐ Do you periodically review your hiring process for improvements and stay up-to-date on new techniques and legal requirements?

APPENDIX A

SAMPLE INTERVIEW QUESTIONS

Listed below is a collection of questions that may be asked during an interview. Remember that all inquiries must be job related.

Work experience

- What do you consider your greatest accomplishment in a work environment and why?
- Why do you think you were successful?
- What is the single most important idea you have contributed to your present job?
- How do you go about making important decisions?
- Describe the relationship between you and your present boss.
- What are your boss's title and functions?
- What are the duties in your present job?
- What percentage of time do you spend on each duty?
- What type of supervision do you have?
- What is the biggest frustration in your present job?
- Describe the reporting structure in your present job.
- With whom do you deal on a regular basis within your office?
- Do you supervise others? How many?
- Describe your style of supervision.
- What do you most like doing in your present job?
- If you had the opportunity to change two things at your present job, what would they be?
- What was the most difficult task you have had to complete?
- If I asked your boss to evaluate your performance, what would they say?
- Why do you wish to leave your present job?

APPENDIX A—SAMPLE INTERVIEW QUESTIONS (Continued)

Education and training

- Have you graduated from high school?
- What was your overall grade point average?
- Do you feel your grades are a fair reflection of your work?
- If not, why not?
- Have you attended college?
- What did you study?
- Have you completed your course of study?
- What courses did you do best in? Why?
- What courses did you have the most trouble with?
- What courses did you dislike the most? Why?
- Were you involved in extracurricular activities? If yes, which ones?
- What did you like best about school?
- Do you feel your education was worthwhile?
- Would you pick the same course of study again?
- How did you happen to change to a different school?

Military service

- Why did you enlist in the military?
- Why did you choose the branch you did?
- What was your rank or grade?
- Did you ever consider making a career in the military?
- Why did you decide against it?
- What type of assignments did you perform in the military?
- Why did you leave the military at the time you did?

The job in question

- Why did you apply for this position?
- What do you know about our company?
- What appeals most to you about this job?
- What strengths do you bring to this position?
- How does this job compare with other positions to which you are applying?
- How does this job fit into your future career plans?
- What did you do on your last job to make yourself more effective?
- If you were hiring someone for this position, what qualities would you look for?
- How does this position compare to positions you have filled in the past?
- If you are hired, what kind of attendance record can we expect?
- Is there anything that will hinder you from getting to work on time?
- What reservations should I have about hiring you?

Personal traits

- Tell me three characteristics about yourself?
- What makes you different than the other candidates?
- What motivates you?
- What are your career goals?
- Why do you think you would be successful in this job?
- What was the best job you ever had? Why?
- Who was the best boss you ever had? Why?
- Do you like working as part of a team?
- What do you consider important in a job?
- Are you most comfortable leading or following? Why?
- Is there anything you'd like to add about yourself that we have not discussed?
- Do you have any questions about the job or our company?

APPENDIX B

STRATEGIES FOR ATTRACTING APPLICANTS

Here are a selection of strategies that have been used successfully by a variety of organizations. While some may appear too bold or unusual at first glance, take a minute to consider how each one might be applied to your recruiting effort.

Ads featuring top workers: Ads with pictures featuring productive employees send the message that your organization cares about its workers. Familiar faces must be recognized and the employees featured will get a charge out of the attention.

Ads in community language: Advertising in English when many in the community speak another language is ill-advised. While many cannot read the ads, it may also offend those who can because they think the company is insensitive.

Appreciation programs: Hold an annual event recognizing employees. Give awards. Have fun. And make sure it is covered in the local press.

Business card applications: While more gimmick than application, these grab the attention of potential applicants. Ask all employees to carry one in their purse or wallet.

Cash awards: Nothing motivates better than cold cash. Publicly reward employees who bring in referrals.

Celebrity hosted events: Ask or hire a local celebrity to host a plant tour, new product roll-out or other event. Once the crowd is attracted, go to work on recruiting employees.

Commuter rail and bus passes: For those in low income areas, providing essentially free commuting can be a significant incentive. Tokens and passes can usually be purchased at quantity discounts.

Competing personnel: Keep an eye on top performers in competing organizations. While you don't want to encourage the pirating of employees, their restlessness may be to your advantage if they're looking for a change.

APPENDIX B—STRATEGIES FOR ATTRACTING APPLICANTS (Continued)

Customer advertisements: Customers who know and use your products can become reliable employees. Make sure they are aware of openings. Posting signs in a store and stuffing bills with position announcements are two effective strategies.

Customer referrals: Ask customers to refer applicants. You might even offer incentives such as discount coupons.

Dead résumé file: Don't throw out those old résumés. Phoning applicants from six months ago may garner some new interest.

Drawings for cash prizes: Consider a program where successful applicants are made eligible for a cash drawing provided they stay a specified period of time.

Full benefits for part-timers: This can be a very attractive to those in single parent situations. While this can be expensive, you can achieve better retention along with loyal workers.

High school and college shepherd program: Develop a program to assist minorities by providing tutoring and financial assistance. In addition, you can provide summer jobs and eventually entice them into working full-time for your firm. This is a long term investment with a long term reward.

Hot air balloons: These generally attract a great amount of attention. Tether one in a parking lot or field outside your plant and recruit those interested.

Interns: High school and college interns provide an excellent source of immediate human resources and an opportunity to see potential employees in action.

Job opportunity brochures: Develop a brochure describing the employment opportunities within your company and make sure that all employees have a few to distribute. When someone says, ''Tell me about your company,'' hand out a brochure.

Job shares: Allow two individuals to share the same position. This can be very attractive to skilled applicants having commitments at home.

Keep in touch with those who leave: Follow up on good employees who leave for other positions. Send them a periodic post-card or note. Former employees may want to come back in the future, and they already know your system.

Layered advertising: Some companies use advertisements that draw applicants in by making a bold statement at the top and then lead into information about the job. One organization, for instance, ran an ad with the words "temporary sanity" at the top to attract those looking for part-time work.

Mobile recruiting vans: Rent a van and set up a mobile recruiting station at the local mall or movie theatre. Find ways to go to the applicants instead of asking them to come to you.

On-site interviews: In the same vein, rent a store front or kiosk in the local mall and solicit applications from passersby.

"Open Air" sessions: Conduct periodic meetings with current employees for the purposes of hashing out concerns and grievances. While these meetings may be quiet at first, employees will open up after a while and speak out. This is also an excellent time to ask staff for ideas on recruiting applicants. Make sure these meetings are reported in the press. A company with an open atmosphere breeds interest.

Outplacement pools: Stay on top of organizations around town that might be downsizing. Ask if you can speak to their employees who are being laid off.

Parking lots: Advertise that you have close-in parking lots for night shifts. This will relieve the apprehension by some that it might be dangerous to work at your company at night.

Part-time workers: Examine whether you need to fill all new openings with full-time workers. Can one or two part-time employees do the same job? Part-timers not only save you money but are easier to find.

Personalized advertisements: Rather than placing the traditional classified advertisement, try a more personalized approach: "We'll miss you, Susan! Susan has been our accounts receivable clerk for the past five years and now she's leaving. She is skilled at handling receivables of up to $300,000 per month, can budget for her department and is able to fill in as bookkeeper when needed. If you think you would like to take Susan's place in this fast-paced, but fun atmosphere, call Bob at 574-7468 before Friday!"

APPENDIX B—STRATEGIES FOR ATTRACTING APPLICANTS

Position for the family: Position your organization as being family oriented. With the return of traditional values, many applicants will find this atmosphere attractive. Making your company more family oriented, of course, has to be a sincere effort.

Posters in foreign languages: Print your recruiting posters and materials in languages of the local community. This demonstrates goodwill and enhances the number of possible applicants.

Promotions with the media: Team up with local radio or television stations to promote the company using gimmicks, contests or drawings. Have staff ready to answer questions and recruit applicants.

Recruiting slogans: Develop a slogan that grabs the attention of the group you are recruiting. The Los Angeles Police Department uses the slogan, ''Be Somebody! Be a Cop!''

Referrals from applicants: Ask applicants for the names and phone numbers of other individuals they know who might also be interested in a job. They might like to work with their friends.

Referrals on applications: Include a space on applications for applicants to list others who might be interested in working for your organization.

Rehire former employees: Be willing to re-hire former employees if they apply. While a few may be undesirable, most will fit right in and already know your systems, which saves training.

Relocation: Consider providing a stipend to a superior candidate to assist with moving expenses. This has been a common practice for hiring executives.

Retiree job bank: Develop a listing of retirees who might be interested in working at their old job from time to time. Companies that have tried this say it works extremely well.

Return postage: Always provide return postage for applications. You don't want to lose good candidates because they don't have the money for a stamp.

School relations: Develop better relations with the schools in your area. They can be a tremendous source of labor and referrals. Offer to make presentations. Contribute equipment and sponsor events and contests. Through these activities, you can develop a positive reputation.

Shared housing: In locales where housing is in short supply, such as resorts, offer shared housing to accommodate new employees and those working temporarily.

Sign-on bonuses: While this has been common practice for executives, the offer of an extra $50 dollars may sway good candidates from taking other positions.

Slang on ads and posters: Build the current slang into recruitment advertising when attracting adolescents. The more they identify with your organization, the more they will apply and tell others.

Sponsored entertainment: Sponsor entertainment, parties and the like to attract applicants. As with any gimmick, it is up to you to recruit interested individuals once they've arrived.

Subsidized housing: In wealthy areas, subsidized housing eases applicant's apprehensions about finding a place to live.

Teacher unions and school districts: Consult with these organizations to locate teachers who are interested in part- or full-time employment during the summer.

Telecommuting: A number of companies have begun to allow certain individuals to work at home and attend meetings in the office. These companies provide the necessary materials and equipment and the employee benefits from not having to commute and can attend to family needs.

Telephone job line: Install a phone line dedicated to announcing current openings. Potential applicants can call the line periodically to check for new positions.

Temporary workers: Consider the use of temporary staff in more than clerical positions. A temporary operations manager can set up a new production line or a marketing manager can roll out a new product without your organization having to hire another full-time person.

Tenure awards: Give awards for those employees who pass certain marks in attendance. McDonalds restaurants begin by recognizing their employees by awarding an attendance pin after the first three months at work.

Toll-free number: Encourage candidates from long distances to phone toll-free. The modest cost of this service is overcome by the goodwill extended to potential applicants.

APPENDIX B—STRATEGIES FOR ATTRACTING APPLICANTS (Continued)

Tours of the site: If your organization is the source of fascination in the community, use this to your advantage. Offer tours on a periodic basis and place a table with applications at the end.

Training for diversity: Train all managers to adapt to the new diversity in the work force. This is becoming an essential skill not only in supervision but more importantly in recruiting.

Training sessions: Some companies offer training courses to potential applicants. The applicants gain by receiving training on particular equipment and the company gets a trained employee if they pass the course.

Two-timing employees: Ask current employees to take on a second job such as custodian or maintenance engineer. In this, you have a reliable employee and this person earns the extra money desired.

Un-retire employees: Approach the retirees of other firms who performed tasks they could perform in your company. Many will be anxious to get back to work, at least part-time.

Van services: Provide van service to employees having to commute through less desirable areas or at night. This provides goodwill and reduces insurance risk.

Visiting executives: Ask your executives to make presentations in the community on the organization's need for qualified people. This information should also be included in any presentations they make to any group. This works especially well if they have achieved some notoriety or fame.

What other ideas can you come up with?

APPENDIX C

BIBLIOGRAPHY AND RESOURCES

Books

Smart Hiring: The Complete Guide to Recruiting Employees
Robert Wendover, 1989
Management Staff Press, Inc.
7500 E. Arapahoe Road
Englewood, Colorado 80112
(800) 227-5510

Robert Half On Hiring
Robert Half, 1985
Crown Publishers, Inc.
1 Park Avenue
New York, NY 10016

The Hiring Handbook
Darlene Orlov, Ed., 1986
Institute for Management
14 Plaza Road
Greenvale, NY 11548

Labor and Employment Law Desk Book
Gordon Jackson, 1986
Prentice-Hall, Inc.
Englewood Cliffs, NJ

Labor and Employment Law: Compliance and Litigation
Frederick T. Golder, 1987
Callaghan & Company
3201 Old Glenview Road
Wilmette, IL 60091

Immigration Employment Compliance Handbook
A.T. Fragomen and S.C. Bell, 1987
Clark Boardman Company
435 Hudson Street
New York, NY 10014

Modern Personnel Forms
Deborah Launer, Rev. 1988
Warren Gorham & Lamont
210 South Street
Boston, MA 02111

The Law of the Workplace: Rights of Employers and Employees
Frederick T. Golder, 1987
Callaghan & Company
3201 Old Glenview Road
Wilmette, IL 60091

Employment Law in the 50 States: A Reference for Employers
CUE/NAM
1331 Pennsylvania Ave. NW
Suite 1500-North Lobby
Washington, DC 20004-1703

Drug Testing Legal Manual
Kevin B. Zeese, 1988
Clark Boardman Company, Ltd.
435 Hudson Street
New York, NY 10014

Employer's Complete Guide to Immigration
Howard David Deutsch, 1987
Prentice Hall Information Services
Paramus, NJ 07652

Your First 30 Days
Elwood Chapman
Crisp Publications

New Employee Orientation
Charles Cadwell
Crisp Publications

Quality Interviewing
Robert Maddux
Crisp Publications

APPENDIX C—BIBLIOGRAPHY AND RESOURCES (Continued)

Current Periodicals

HR Magazine
Society for Human Resource Management
606 N. Washington Street
Alexandria, VA 22314
(703) 548-3440

HR News
Society for Human Resource Management
606 N. Washington Street
Alexandria, VA 22314
(703) 548-3440

Personnel Journal
P.O. Box 2440
Costa Mesa, CA 92628
(714) 751-1883

Boardroom Reports
Box 1026
Millburn, NJ 07041

Inc.
38 Commercial Wharf
Boston, MA 02110
(617) 227-4700

Employment Practice Reference Sources
Bureau of National Affairs
1231 25th Street NW
Washington, DC 20037
(301) 258-1033

Bureau of Law and Business
64 Wall Street
Madison, CT 06443
1-800-553-4569
(203) 245-7448 (CT)

Commerce Clearing House
4025 W. Peterson Ave.
Chicago, IL 60646
(312) 583-8500

Dartnell, Inc.
4660 Ravenswood Ave.
Chicago, IL 60640
(312) 561-4000

EEOC
Publications Department
2401 "E" Street, NW
Washington, DC 20507
(202) 634-6922

Personnel Forms

Amsterdam Printing and Litho
Wallins Corner Road
Amsterdam, NY 12010
1-800-833-6231
1-800-342-6116 (NY State)

Dartnell, Inc.
4660 Ravenswood Ave.
Chicago, IL 60640
1-800-612-5463
(312) 561-4000 (IL)

Selectform, Inc.
Box 3045
Freeport, NY 11520
(516) 623-0400

Testing

E.F. Wonderlic & Associates
820 Frontage Road
Northfield, IL 60093
(312) 446-8900

ETS Test Collection
Educational Testing Service
Princeton, NJ 08541
(609) 921-9000

London House, Inc.
1550 Northwest Highway
Park Ridge, IL 60068
1-800-323-5923
(312) 298-7311 (IL)

John E. Reid & Associates
233 N. Michigan, Suite 1614
Chicago, IL 60601
1-800-621-4553
(312) 938-9200

Stanton Corporation
417 South Dearborn
Chicago, IL 60605
1-800-621-4552
(312) 922-0970

Employment History Verification

Fidelifacts
50 Broadway
New York, NY 10004
1-800-223-3140
(212) 425-1520 (NY)

Equifax Services, Inc.
1600 Peachtree Street, NW
Atlanta, GA 30309
1-800-327-5932

Verified Credentials, Inc.
4010 West 65th Street
Minneapolis, MN 55435
(612) 431-1811

NOTES

NOTES

NOTES

NOTES

NOTES

NOW AVAILABLE FROM
CRISP PUBLICATIONS

Books • Videos • CD Roms • Computer-Based Training Products

If you enjoyed this book, we have great news for you. There are over 200 books available in the *50-Minute*™ Series. To request a free full-line catalog, contact your local distributor or Crisp Publications, Inc., 1200 Hamilton Court, Menlo Park, CA 94025. Our toll-free number is 800-442-7477.

Subject Areas Include:

Management

Human Resources

Communication Skills

Personal Development

Marketing/Sales

Organizational Development

Customer Service/Quality

Computer Skills

Small Business and Entrepreneurship

Adult Literacy and Learning

Life Planning and Retirement

CRISP WORLDWIDE DISTRIBUTION

English language books are distributed worldwide. Major international distributors include:

ASIA/PACIFIC

Australia/New Zealand: In Learning, PO Box 1051 Springwood QLD, Brisbane, Australia 4127
Telephone: 7-3841-1061, Facsimile: 7-3841-1580   ATTN: Messrs. Gordon

Singapore: Graham Brash (Pvt) Ltd. 32, Gul Drive, Singapore 2262
Telephone: 65-861-1336, Facsimile: 65-861-4815   ATTN: Mr. Campbell

CANADA

Reid Publishing, Ltd., Box 69559-109 Thomas Street, Oakville, Ontario Canada L6J 7R4.
Telephone: (905) 842-4428, Facsimile: (905) 842-9327   ATTN: Mr. Reid

Trade Book Stores: Raincoast Books, 8680 Cambie Street, Vancouver, British Columbia, Canada V6P 6M9.
Telephone: (604) 323–7100, Facsimile: 604-323-2600   ATTN: Ms. Laidley

EUROPEAN UNION

England: Flex Training, Ltd. 9-15 Hitchin Street, Baldock, Hertfordshire, SG7 6A, England
Telephone: 1-462-896000, Facsimile: 1-462-892417   ATTN: Mr. Willetts

INDIA

Multi-Media HRD, Pvt., Ltd., National House, Tulloch Road, Appolo Bunder, Bombay, India 400-039
Telephone: 91-22-204-2281, Facsimile: 91-22-283-6478   ATTN: Messrs. Aggarwal

MIDDLE EAST

United Arab Emirates: Al-Mutanabbi Bookshop, PO Box 71946, Abu Dhabi
Telephone: 971-2-321-519, Facsimile: 971-2-317-706   ATTN: Mr. Salabbai

SOUTH AMERICA

Mexico: Grupo Editorial Iberoamerica, Serapio Rendon #125, Col. San Rafael, 06470 Mexico, D.F.
Telephone: 525-705-0585, Facsimile: 525-535-2009   ATTN: Señor Grepe

SOUTH AFRICA

Alternative Books, Unit A3 Sanlam Micro Industrial Park, Hammer Avenue STRYDOM Park, Randburg, 2194 South Africa
Telephone: 2711 792 7730, Facsimile: 2711 792 7787   ATTN: Mr. de Haas